LITTLE GARY'S JOURNEY

LITTLE GARY'S
Journey

An autobiography in story form

G. M. TRUJILLO

Copyright © 2019 Gary M. Trujillo

All rights reserved. No part of this publication may be reproduced, distributed, or transmitted in any form or by any means, including photocopying, recording, or other electronic or mechanical methods, without the prior written permission of the publisher, except in the case of brief quotations embodied in critical reviews and certain other noncommercial uses permitted by copyright law. For permission requests, write to the publisher, addressed "Attention: Permissions Coordinator," at the address below.

ISBN: 978-0-578-43727-9
Library of Congress Control Number: 2019900280

Any references to historical events, real people, or real places are used fictitiously. Names, characters, and places are products of the author's imagination.

Cover design by Jon Sternoff & Don Trujillo
Interior design by Jennifer Sugden

Printed by DiggyPOD, Inc., in the United States of America

First printing edition 2019

KLET & J LLC, Publisher
733 NE 204th St.
Shoreline, WA 98155

To my brother, Paul

Prologue — 11

chapter one
Candy Corn — 17

chapter two
Hostess CupCake — 41

chapter three
Beans — 55

chapter four
Final Days — 73

chapter five
The Move — 90

chapter six
Establishing Roots — 104

chapter seven
Moving Forward — 122

chapter eight
The Call — 139

chapter nine
The Last Mile — 163

Epilogue — 189

Acknowledgments — 193

Prologue

It was Gary's last day on the job before retiring from government service of twenty-seven years, including serving in the military, as he sat in his plush velvet swivel armchair in his office on the seventeenth floor of the Rainier Tower building, overlooking the city's skyscrapers, Mount Rainier silhouetted in the background, and the Puget Sound gushing against the waterfront. Gazing out over the city's amazing scenery, Gary felt a sense of melancholy, blended with joy and excitement about his plans for the next chapter of his life. He thought it necessary to stay active once retired, so his plan was to start his own company as a small-business consultant specializing in government contracting and start-ups. He had learned so much during his professional career and didn't want any of his skills to go untested. Then he began reflecting back on his childhood and life's long journey that had brought him to where he was now sitting—a journey spanning sixty-plus years paved with moments of sadness and happiness, and many challenges.

Yes, it has been a long journey, he thought, *since those early years growing up poor in the slums of Denver's inner city, living in dilapidated low-income dwellings and government housing projects, to where I'm living today. I believe it was during that early time of my life that shaped who I am and instilled in me the courage and fortitude to pursue the better aspects of life. Complemented by my childhood friends, the influence of family, later friends and relatives along the way, the guidance of the Catholic Church, and the loving support of my wife, Nancy, of forty-four years, who I met in high school; all of these factors contributed immensely to my well-being.*

Gary could still remember the stern but loving voice of his mother as she leaned out the window that warm summer day and instructed him and his older sister, Margaret, to stay near the front porch; the comforting words of Miss Tiger, his second-grade teacher, when she consoled him during that moment of heartache and disappointment as they sat on the floor next to his coat locker at school; the sound advice of Officer Young, the neighborhood policeman, who used to warn all the neighborhood kids of the dangers of street life; his father's disciplinary manner manifesting as the only way he knew of showing his love toward his wife and seven children; the nuns and priests whose spiritual guidance, which at the time seemed harsh and uncaring, was a blessing that guided him through the perils of life. Most memorable, however, of Gary's childhood, was the loving presence of his mother, whose quiet demeanor spoke volumes of God's love.

While Gary was remembering the past, a loud voice

echoed from another office, asking if he was going to answer his phone, which had been ringing off the hook for the past few minutes. Not responding, Gary reached from his comfortable chair and picked up the receiver, answering, "SBA, may I help you? Oh, hi, sweetheart. Yeah, I'm sorry. I was sort of daydreaming."

"Wait, don't tell me. It was about *Little Gary's Journey*," she said.

"Yeah, how'd you know?" Gary asked rhetorically.

"Well, which part of *Little Gary's Journey* were you *sort of* daydreaming about?" quipped his wife. "Was it 'Candy Corn,' 'Beans,' when we met in high school, or when you had all those jobs?" Now they could both look back on these moments and joke about them, but at the time, it was nothing to joke about.

"Well, actually, I was thinking back about my entire life, from age four to this moment in time, and what I should incorporate in my book. So far, as you know, I've only finished writing five chapters covering Little Gary from the time he was playing Cowboys in the front of his house to when he and his family moved into the housing projects. I want my book to be an autobiography in story form from childhood to adulthood, covering all of life's ups and downs, including the many hardships, moments of heartbreak, disappointments, and of course accomplishments, which would have been impossible to achieve without your loving support."

"So, when are you going to stop daydreaming about Little Gary's journey and finish what you started writing years ago? You know how I feel about the stories you have written: they're beautiful and heartwarming, and you need to continue, if not for your own gratification, then for our grandchildren and future great-grandchildren. I think it would be a wonderful legacy to leave them. They need to know who we were, the struggles we faced, and how we overcame them. Now stop daydreaming, and maybe next time you'll answer the phone after two rings instead of fifty," she ended with, jokingly.

Gary had always talked about writing down his life experiences, growing up poor in the slums and housing projects in the inner city and the obstacles he faced striving to make a better life for his family, but he kept putting it off.

"Yeah, it would be nice to share our life experiences with the grandchildren."

"Then do it," his wife said. "Just sit down at the computer and finish what you started thirty years ago."

To his wife, everything seemed so matter-of-fact, black-and-white. She was a no-nonsense woman who hated procrastination. If something had to be done, she would do it. She didn't like wasting time, nor did she particularly care to think about the past or the future for that matter. What mattered most to her was the present.

She was very supportive and encouraging of her husband. Like the time he converted an oversized room into a bedroom and a utility room. And she always marveled at how he would phrase words when creating birthday or anniversary cards for family and friends, or when he would write letters on a particular subject.

She had faith in her husband and knew he was capable of doing whatever he put his mind to. After all, she'd known him since they entered high school at the age of fourteen.

"Oh, before I forget why I called, I need you to stop off at the store after work and pick up five packages of corn tortillas. I invited the kids over for enchiladas tomorrow so we can celebrate your retirement."

"Will do," Gary said. "Now may I go back to my daydreaming? I still have a lot of remembering to do."

"Sure, as long as you don't forget to bring home the tortillas. By the way, do you ever get any work done? Love you."

"Ditto," Gary replied.

For the balance of the morning, Gary sat at the computer, preparing a farewell letter to his co-workers, though his childhood memories still faded in and out, along with how much he had accomplished during his lifetime. Although in the back of his mind he still questioned whether he should write about his life; excuses and self-doubt seemed to clog his thinking and made him wonder if he was capable of such an arduous task.

That evening, during dinner, the topic of Gary's life journey took center stage as it had on other occasions, only this time there was a sense of urgency in his voice that had not been there before. He could still visualize the bag of candy corn scattered all over the street as he sat on the curb crying when he was just four years old. Then when he was seven, and he could see himself in the schoolyard, leaning up against the redbrick wall, holding on tightly to his brown lunch bag, waiting for the school bell to ring so by lunchtime he could eat his Hostess CupCake. His memories started flashing through his mind at high speed as he recalled his years in school, the jobs he held, his time in the army, and the social revolution of the 1960s. He remembered the minority students and community supporters, demonstrating against restrictive admissions policies at major college campuses around the country, which adversely affected their enrollment, where he himself was a participant at the university at which he worked as an administrator overseeing the recruitment of Chicano students.

This time Gary was finally determined to bring Little Gary's journey to life, excited to resume his writing, that is, just as soon as he finished eating the beans he had for dinner that evening. "I love beans," he said.

Candy Corn
chapter one

It was a warm summer evening, still early enough to enjoy the remaining daylight hours. Four-year-old Gary, who would be entering kindergarten in the fall, sat on the front porch trying to separate a cowboy pistol he'd found in the vacant lot across the alley from the housing terraces where he lived with his parents and six siblings. After struggling with his toy pistol for several minutes, he managed to pull it apart. Now he had two tin pistols, one for each pocket he pretended was a holster.

"Bang, bang," he shouted, rapidly drawing his pistols from his holsters and shooting at passing cars he imagined were outlaws being chased by the sheriff and his posse. "Bang, bang," he shouted again, shooting his pistols as he hid behind the porch post as if exchanging gunfire with the bad guys. He then jumped off the porch into the tall weeds just below the living room window. Seconds later, he slowly raised his head, looked around, and crawled back onto the porch, quietly saying to himself, "It's all clear. I musta got 'em all." Then, proudly raising both pistols to his lips in a single motion, he blew the imaginary trail of smoke from the gun barrels and placed them back into his holsters.

With yet an hour of daylight still left to play, Little Gary jumped on his makeshift broomstick horse and rode up and down the sidewalk, yelling, "Giddyap, giddyap!"

As Little Gary galloped toward the other end of the house, away from the front porch, he could hear someone calling him in a low voice, "Gary, Gary, come here a minute." It was his older sister, six-year-old Margaret, whom he called Maggie.

"What do you want?" he said loudly.

"Shush," she said. "Be quiet and come over here."

"I'm playing Cowboys, can't you see? What do you want?"

"Do you want some candy?" she whispered.

"What kind?" he asked.

"Just come over here and I'll tell you."

"Tell me first."

"Well, if you don't want any, I'll eat it all myself," Margaret threatened.

"Okay, okay, I'm coming," Little Gary said as he trotted closer to the side of the house near the alley from where his sister was calling. "Okay, where's the candy?" he asked skeptically.

"It's at the store. We have to go to the store to get it."

"Heck no, I'm not crossing the street. You know what Mommy said about not ever crossing the street by ourselves."

"It's okay, it's okay; we're not alone, we're together," his sister assured him. "We're only going to be gone a few minutes. We'll be right back, and Mother won't even know we were gone. I promise," Margaret said believingly. "Now come on, give me your hand."

Reluctantly, Little Gary stretched out his arm and asked his sister, "What kind of candy we gonna get?" as his dark eyes lit up.

"Candy corn," Margaret answered. "Now be quiet and don't say anything if Mother sees us and asks where we're going. I'll do the talking," his sister instructed.

As Little Gary and Margaret walked past the front of the house, holding hands, their mother, who was ironing clothes in the living room, leaned out the window and asked where they were going.

"Nowhere, Mother, we're just walking and talking," Margaret politely replied.

"You stay in front of the house and look after your brother, you hear?"

"Yes, Mother, I will," Margaret said, smiling.

Gazing out at the children, Little Gary's mother thought how wonderful it would be to live in a neighborhood away from the busy streets and in a house all their own with a large fenced-in yard where the children could safely play. She always worried when the children played in front of the house, but knew she couldn't keep them cooped up indoors all day. She simply left them in God's hands. "*Oh Dios mío,* please protect my family," she whispered.

"Is she still looking?" Margaret asked Little Gary.

"Is who still looking?" Little Gary snapped back.

"Is Mother still looking? Who did you think I was talking about?"

"Well, you didn't say. Yes, Mommy's still looking at us."

"Okay, let's turn around again and walk toward the house, then when she's not looking, we'll turn around and run to the store really fast—so be ready."

Seconds later, Margaret pulled his arm and said, "Okay, she's gone; let's run!" But before he could say anything, they were at the corner of the block, ready to cross the street.

"Okay, hold on tight," Margaret said. "And as soon as it's clear, we're going to run across the street, okay?"

"Okay, I hear you. But this time don't pull my arm so hard; you almost pulled it off. I think you broke it cuz it feels loose," said Little Gary while trying to catch his breath.

"All right then, give me your other arm. Now get ready." After looking in both directions, Margaret again pulled on his arm and together they ran as fast as their legs could carry them.

"Now you broke my other arm," he said once they got to the other side of the street.

"Oh, stop complaining, you little baby."

"You're the baby," he said quietly as he hugged both his arms close to his chest.

Once inside the store, they walked directly to the candy stand where Mr. Straight, the store owner, was sitting behind the counter, reading the newspaper.

"What'll you kids have?" Mr. Straight asked. "Does your mother know you're here?"

"Oh yes, Mr. Straight, she does," Margaret replied. "Huh, Gary?"

"Uh-huh," Little Gary said, looking down at the floor.

"Okay, what's it going to be?" Mr. Straight asked.

"Well, let me see," Margaret said as if she were undecided.

Very quietly Little Gary said, "I thought you said we were gonna get candy corn?"

"We are, but let's look around first. We may want to buy something else."

"But I don't want something else," he said angrily. "You told me we were gonna get candy corn and that's what I want."

"Okay, okay," Margaret said, somewhat frustrated. "But what about some licorice, that looks pretty good. Or jelly beans. Oh I know, some lemon drops, the really big ones. How does that sound?" she asked Little Gary.

"I don't want any of that other stuff," he said in a loud voice. "I want candy corn. That's my favorite kind of candy."

"Come on, kids, I don't have all day. What's it going to be?" Mr. Straight asked.

"Maggie," Little Gary said under his breath while nudging her. "I think he's getting mad."

"Okay, okay," Margaret said, even more frustrated. "We'll get the candy corn!" Though still not giving up, she continued, "Maybe you will change your mind if you see something else you like. What other things do you like, Gary?"

"Well, my favorite in the whole wide world is Hostess CupCakes. I really love Hostess CupCakes. I could eat them all day," Gary said, licking his lips.

"Well, we don't have enough money for Hostess CupCakes, so stick to candy."

"Then I still want candy corn, nothing else. Do you

hear me?"

"Yes, I hear you. What about some taffy? That's almost like candy corn," Margaret said while still trying to convince Little Gary to try something else.

By now, Little Gary, very agitated, screamed out, "If you don't buy candy corn, I'm telling Mommy you dragged me to the store with you!"

"All right already, stop screaming, I'll buy candy corn," Margaret said as she finally gave in to Gary's persistence.

"Well, you guys, have you made up your mind what you want to buy?" Mr. Straight asked.

Very reluctantly, Margaret replied, "We'll have five cents' worth of candy corn, please."

"Five cents it is," Mr. Straight repeated as he scooped up the candy corn and put it in a little brown bag, nearly filling it to the brim.

"Well, Gary, are you happy now?" Margaret snapped as she handed him the bag of candy corn.

"Yup," Little Gary said with a smile as they walked toward the door.

"Be careful crossing the street, kids," Mr. Straight said.

"Thank you, we will," Margaret responded.

Leaving the store, Little Gary beamed with joy while holding on tightly to the bag of candy corn and humming his favorite tune "Hey Baba Reba," a song he heard on the radio that for some reason stuck with him, and which he would sing or hum whenever he got excited or felt overjoyed. Like the time he was in the alley playing Cowboys when the neighbor's dog crawled under the fence and surprised him with his rapid barking. Little Gary just stood there frozen in one spot and started singing as fast as he could: "Hey Baba Reba, hey Baba Reba, hey Baba Reba." He sang so fast and loud that the little dog got scared and hightailed it back down the alley, under the fence to his own yard.

"Come on, Gary, give me your hand; we got to get back home before Mother finds out we were gone," Margaret said as they walked to the end of the corner block preparing to cross the street. "And hold on tightly because we may have to run for it, and don't drop the candy corn."

"Okay, but don't break my arm again," Little Gary said.

Just as Margaret and Gary stepped off the curb, a loud startling scream echoed in the air from across the street: "Watch out!" followed by a loud screeching noise.

"What the . . . ," said Mr. Straight as he ran out of the store. "Oh my God" were the next words from his mouth.

At that moment, a passerby who had witnessed the incident shouted at Mr. Straight, "Quick, call an ambulance!"

Meanwhile, at home, their mother was straightening up around the house when she heard a loud knocking at the front door and a frantic voice calling out "*Comadre, comadre*, come quickly, Margaret and Gary were in an accident."

"*Oh Dios mío!*" cried their mother as she ran to open the door. "*¿Qué pasó?*" she asked Mrs. Martinez, her next-door neighbor, who just happened to be taking her daughter for a walk when the accident occurred.

"Mr. Straight yelled out to me from down the block to call you; that Margaret and Gary were involved in an accident."

Without saying another word, their mother yelled out to her eldest daughters, Lucinda and Frances, to watch the twins (Danny and Donny) and Paul, that she would be right back, then dashed out the front door. Running as fast as she could to the end of the corner block, she could see flashing red and blue lights blinking off and on. As she reached the street corner, a crowd of onlookers was huddled on the edge of the sidewalk, blocking her view of the accident. She pushed her way through the crowd and ran into the street.

There were police cars blocking the intersection and a policeman redirecting traffic. In the middle of the intersection was an ambulance with its flashing lights circling round and round.

"Wait a minute, lady," yelled a policeman. "Where do you think you're going? Get back on the sidewalk and away from this area; there's been an accident."

"I know, I know, Officer, my children are the ones who are involved. I need to see them. Let me see my children," she demanded. "Are they all right?" she asked hysterically.

"Ma'am, ma'am, please calm down; your children are fine," the police officer said in a soothing voice. "What is your name, ma'am?" the officer asked.

"Mrs. Trujillo. It's Mrs. Trujillo," she repeated. "We live just up the street. Now may I see my children?"

"It's okay, Mac," another policeman from across the street called out to his partner, "you can let her through."

"Okay, Mrs. Trujillo, you may cross now. Sergeant Robles will want to talk to you. He's the officer with the clipboard sitting on the curb, talking to your son."

"Thank you, Officer," she said as she rushed over to the other side of the street.

No sooner had his mother approached Sergeant Robles when Little Gary jumped up from the curb and ran into his mother's arms, crying uncontrollably.

"Mom . . . Mom . . . Mommy, a, a truck, a truck hit us and uh, uh, knocked us down on, on the street and, and ran over us and, and all our candy corn spilled all over, over the street and we, we didn't even get to eat any."

"Oh, *mijo*, are you all right? Are you hurt?" his mother asked lovingly.

"My, my pants got torn and, and I, I got scratches all, all over me. But, but Maggie really got hurt cause she, she was under a truck and now she's in the ambalance. Is she gonna die?"

"Ma'am, the children are fine," interjected Sergeant Robles. "Your daughter is in the ambulance and will be taken to Emergency General. According to the paramedics, she may have a minor concussion, but they won't know for sure until they get her to the hospital. As for your son, he's a little shaken up and has a few scratches but otherwise doing fine. Still, we need to also take him to the hospital just for precautionary sake. Officer Young will take you and your son to the hospital and then see to it you get home once your children are seen by a doctor."

Still sniffling, Little Gary asked, "Mommy, are, are you gonna be mad? Mag, Maggie said we, we could cross the street and, and go to the store to buy uh, uh, some candy corn. She had some money and made, made me go with her."

"No, sweetheart, I'm not mad. I was just worried that something terrible happened, but now I'm happy that you and your sister are okay. But didn't I tell you and Margaret not to leave the front of the house?" she scolded.

"Yes, but, but Maggie said it was okay."

"Well, you both could have really gotten hurt. Don't you ever do something like that again, do you understand me?" she said as she lovingly pulled Little Gary closer to her.

"Uh-huh, I, I will never do, do that again. Are you gonna tell Daddy on us?"

"Everything is going to be all right, honey," she said while trying to console him without answering him. "Don't worry about anything."

"I'd like to see my daughter now, Officer Robles," she asked while walking toward the ambulance.

"Ma'am, you will have to wait until she is taken to the hospital. You'll be able to see her there. Don't worry though, your daughter is going to be fine," Sergeant Robles assured her. "Now, please go with Officer Young."

"Thank you, Officer."

"Okay, little man," Officer Young said, referring to Little Gary. "Are you ready to go for a ride in my police car?"

"Are weeeee . . . going to jail?" stuttered Little Gary.

"No, I'm not taking you to jail. I'm taking you to the hospital so the doctor can check to see if you broke any bones in that little body of yours, and your mother is coming with us so she can be with you and your sister. Okay?"

"Uh-huh," uttered Little Gary, still a little shaken as he held on to his mother's hand while they walked to the patrol car. Just as they were getting into the back seat, Little Gary cried out, "My guns! Where are my guns? I don't have my guns!"

"What are you talking about, Gary?" his mother asked in a somewhat startled manner.

"My guns, I lost my guns."

"What guns? What on earth are you talking about?"

"Are these them?" asked Officer Young as he handed Little Gary the two halves of the toy cowboy pistol.

"Yes, yes, that's them," he said excitedly, and placed each half of the toy pistol into his front pockets. "These are my holsters," he said.

"Gee, I only have one holster and one gun," Officer Young said, playing along.

"Well, maybe you can break yours in half like I did, then you could have two guns," said Little Gary as he went through his quick-draw routine.

"Okay, Little Cowboy, you can finish practicing drawing your pistols at the hospital. We need to leave now before it closes."

"The hospital doesn't close. It stays open all day and all night for when people get hurt," Little Gary smartly replied.

"Come on, up you go, Little Cowboy," Officer Young said as he lifted Little Gary up and placed him in the back seat of his patrol car. Once they drove off, his mother asked Officer Young how the accident happened.

Slightly turning back, keeping his eyes on the road, he replied, "Well, ma'am, according to an eyewitness, your son and daughter were standing at the corner near Straight's Grocery Store, waiting until it was clear to cross the street and after looking both ways proceeded to cross. Then, as they neared the middle of the street, a truck suddenly came out of nowhere and struck the children."

"According to this witness," Officer Young continued, "your daughter instinctively pushed your son off to the side of the road. Unfortunately for your daughter though, she ended up on the other side of the street after the impact of the truck. No telling what would have happened to your son had she not acted quickly as she did. What an amazing act," he added.

"The witness stated that the driver of the truck did not come to a complete stop at the stop sign as he turned the corner, nor was he looking in the direction of his turn. Once he realized what he had done, however, he came to an immediate stop and got out of his truck and ran over to the other side of the street, where your daughter was lying against the curb."

"Just about that time, the eyewitness yelled to the store owner to call for an ambulance. My partner and I got the call and arrived at the scene minutes before the ambulance arrived since we were on patrol nearby. And that's about it in a nutshell," Officer Young concluded.

"By the way, how's your son doing back there? He's been pretty quiet."

"Oh, he's fine," she said. "He dozed off. This has been a very traumatic experience for him."

"Yeah, I bet it has," said Officer Young. "And what a talkative little boy you have. Before you arrived, and after we were able to calm him down, since he was pretty shaken up, your son was talking a mile a minute and wanted to know why the man in the truck ran over him and his sister and if Sergeant Robles was going to take the truck driver to jail and throw away the keys. Then he asked Sergeant Robles if he could pick up the candy corn and trade it in for another bag since he and his sister didn't get a chance to eat any of it."

While Officer Young continued describing Little Gary's actions, his mother listened silently while holding her son's head gently on her lap and stroking his curly black locks, marveling at how courageous her daughter was in protecting her brother from serious injury.

"Well, we're here, Mrs. Trujillo," Officer Young said as he pulled up to the emergency entrance of Emergency General Hospital.

"Wake up, honey," his mother whispered softly in his ear. "We're at the hospital."

Rubbing his eyes, Little Gary said, "Mommy, where we at? Where we going? How come it's dark?"

"Honey, we're at the hospital. Don't you remember what happened?"

"Uh-huh," he replied with a yawn.

"Okay, Little Cowboy, let's go ask the doctor to look you over to see if you're still going to be able to ride your horse and shoot all the outlaws," Officer Young playfully said to Little Gary as they got out of the patrol car.

While not responding to his playfulness, Little Gary turned to his mother and said, "I want a go home. I don't like it here. Let's go home, let's go home," he kept repeating as he pulled on his mother's arm in the opposite direction of the hospital's emergency entrance.

"It's okay, honey, everything is going to be fine," she tried assuring him. "It will just take a few minutes, then we can go home. But first the doctor has to look at your scratches and get you all cleaned up, then we can go see Margaret and be with her while the doctor takes care of her. Okay?"

"No, I don't wanna be here. I wanna go home now. She could stay here, then come home tomorrow in the bus."

"We can't let her stay in the hospital; she needs to go home with us, so let's go get her. Okay, honey?" Still trying to calm him down, his mother said, "Did you know that Margaret pushed you away from the truck so you wouldn't get hurt?"

"I don't know. I just wanna go home," he insisted as he continued to pull on her arm in a direction away from the hospital.

"Say, Little Cowboy," intervened Officer Young, "how would you like to turn on the siren in my patrol car?"

Immediately, Little Gary's dark olive eyes lit up as he yelled out, "Oh, wow! Mommy, I get to turn on the siren in the cop car."

"But first," Officer Young said, "we have to go inside the hospital to get you looked at and then get your sister, so she could see you turn on the siren. Okay?"

"Mommy, let's go, hurry," Little Gary said as he turned toward the hospital emergency entrance, pulling his mother with him. "Hey, Baba Reba; hey, Baba Reba. I get to do the siren," he sang as they entered the hospital.

"Have a seat in the waiting room, Mrs. Trujillo, and I'll

inquire about your daughter and let admittance know of your son's situation," said Officer Young as he walked toward the hospital admittance desk.

"Thank you, Officer Young," she said as she and Little Gary sat down on a long, narrow wooden bench propped up against a wall in an overcrowded waiting room. *My, what a lot of people,* she thought as she looked around the room. *It's so sad to see all these people here. I wonder if some of them have been waiting a long time to be seen.*

"Mommy, Mommy, I have to go wee-wee really bad," Little Gary said while placing both hands between his legs.

"Okay, let's go find the bathroom. Can you hold it?"

"I don't think so. It hurts to walk. I have to go now," he said, squirming.

"Come on, there's restroom at the end of the hallway," his mother said.

As they walked toward the restroom, Little Gary turned to his mother and said, "This is the girl's toilet. I can't go in there."

"It's okay, honey," his mother assured him. "It's also for little boys. Now come on."

Reluctantly, Little Gary followed his mother into the bathroom while looking around to see if any other little boys were there. Once inside the restroom, he asked out loud, "Well, where are the little boys? I don't see any. You said this was for little boys."

"Gary, it's okay; you could go here, there's nobody watching."

When they returned to the waiting room, Officer Young

informed his mother that Margaret was in the emergency room with the doctor; she didn't have a concussion after all but would require a few stitches just above her forehead. But she was not to worry, and the doctor would be able to see Little Gary in a few minutes.

As time passed, a few minutes turned into an hour and an hour turned into two hours, by which time Little Gary had fallen fast asleep on the hard wooden bench. Then, just as the hands on the clock struck 8:00 p.m., a loud voice could be heard over the intercom. "Mrs. Trallo, Mrs. Trallo, please report to admittance."

"Honey, wake up," his mother said, gently poking his fragile little body. "It's our turn to go see the doctor." It had been several hours since the accident, and Little Gary was exhausted as was his mother, so they walked tiredly over to the admittance desk.

"The doctor will see you now, Mrs. Trallo," said the admittance clerk. "He's in room A23, down the hall on the right. Please fill out these forms and have the doctor sign them, then drop them off here at the desk on your way out."

Little Gary's mother thanked the admittance clerk, then before proceeding down a long stretch of hallway lined with people on both sides waiting to be seen, she very politely said to the admittance clerk, "For future reference, ma'am, the name is pronounced 'Truheo.' The *j* sounds like 'he' and the letter *l*'s are silent."

"Okay, thank you for that," the admittance clerk said, somewhat unapologetic.

"Well, you must be the Little Cowboy everybody's talking about," a young intern said as he greeted Little

Gary and his mother. "Mrs. Trujillo, I'm Doctor Joseph. I hope I pronounced your name right."

"Yes, Doctor, you did. Thank you."

"I just came from treating your daughter. Sorry for the long wait. She had a deep gash on her forehead and required several stitches. She's doing fine, though, and resting in the next room; she should be ready to go home once I finish examining your son."

"Thank you, Doctor," said his mother. "I'm relieved to hear that."

"Please have a seat, Mrs. Trujillo. I'll only be a few minutes with your son. Okay, Little Cowboy, see if you could jump up onto this table so that I can take a look at you. I understand your body is full of scratches. What happened? Did your horse throw you for a loop?" the doctor said, kidding.

"No, my sister and me got run over by a truck and our candy corn spilled all over the street and we didn't even get to eat any," Little Gary explained.

"Wow, that's terrible," said the doctor. "I thought maybe your horse bucked you off."

"I don't have a horse. I have a broomstick I use for my horse when I'm playing Cowboys. And a broomstick can't buck me off cuz it's a stick."

"Oh, I see. A stick for a horse, huh. Well, before I can look at your scratches, you will have to remove your pistols from your pockets and put them over on the table next to your mother."

"Them are my holsters," Little Gary said as if offended.

"Oh, I'm sorry. Then remove your two pistols from your holsters so they don't get in the way when I'm examining you. Okay?"

"Okay," Little Gary said, "but I want them back."

After the examination the doctor said to his mother that he appeared to be in good shape; there was nothing to be concerned about. He only had a few scratches and bruises, but he may feel some discomfort and soreness for a day or so, then would be good as new.

"Did you hear what the doctor said, Gary?"

But all Little Gary could think of was putting his toy pistols back into his "holsters" and resuming his fantasy.

"May I see my daughter now, Doctor?" said his mother.

"Yes, of course. I'll go get her."

"Gary, the doctor went to get Margaret, then we can go home. Are you ready to go home?" she asked.

"Uh-huh," he said, without really paying attention to what his mother was saying.

A few minutes later Margaret walked into their room with her head fully bandaged and lowered toward the floor. As she looked up toward her mother, tears filled her eyes.

"Mother, I'm so sorry I disobeyed you," Margaret said sorrowfully. "But it wasn't our fault we . . ." But before she could say another word, her mother rushed over and put her arms around her daughter and held her tightly for several seconds.

"Sweetheart, I'm just happy you're okay. How do you feel?"

"My head hurts a little. Could we just go home now?"

"Yes, sweetheart, we're going home."

Little Gary, in the meantime, had walked out into the hallway and was talking to the nurses, telling them all about getting run over by a truck and dropping his candy corn all over the street before he could eat any, and that he was going to be able to turn on the siren in the police car on his way home. Then he told the nurses about how he made two cowboy pistols out of one toy gun. Then, as an afterthought, he said, "Oh! I'm gonna start school too!" The nurses just stood there amazed at how talkative and animated he was.

"Come on, Gary, we're going home," Margaret called to him.

"Okay, I gotta go now," Little Gary said to the nurses. "I gotta go turn on the siren in the cop car. As Little Gary turned toward his sister, he said, "Gee, Maggie, you look like a zombie."

"Well, you don't look any better yourself. So there," she shot back.

"Well, Mrs. Trujillo, I'm glad everything turned out fine," said Doctor Joseph. "The kids were very lucky. Someone must have been looking out over them."

"There was, Doctor. Yes, there was," his mother said with a smile. "Is there anything I need to do before we leave?"

"Yes, Mrs. Trujillo, just take these release forms back to the admittance desk on your way out. Thank you."

"No, thank you, Doctor. Given how busy things look around here, I'm much appreciative for the care given my children. Thanks again."

"You're welcome, Mrs. Trujillo. Bye, Margaret, make sure you get plenty of rest when you get home so your stitches can heal. Okay?"

"I will, Doctor," Margaret answered.

"As for you, Little Cowboy, take care of your mother and sister. And remember, I don't want to see you here again. You hear?"

Not paying attention to Doctor Joseph, Little Gary walked down the hallway, ahead of his mother and sister, with his hands clutched to his toy pistols as if he were ready to pull them out of his holsters at any moment. After handing in the release forms, his mother walked over to where Officer Young was seated and thanked him for waiting and apologized for it taking so long.

"Don't think anything of it, Mrs. Trujillo," Officer Young said. "My shift ended an hour ago, so I'm somewhat free at the moment. Unless of course I'm faced with an emergency, which sometimes happens. How are the kids doing? Is everything all right?" he asked.

"Yes, thank God. Nothing serious. Margaret required a few stitches, and Gary escaped with a few bruises and scratches. But other than that, everything turned out fine."

"Well, that's nice to hear," said Officer Young. "It could have been much worse," he added.

"Yes, it could have," she replied. "Could we leave now? I'd like to get the kids home. It's getting late."

"Yes, of course," said Officer Young. "It's been a long, tiring day, I bet."

"It has," their mother answered.

Suddenly out of nowhere a loud voice screeched out, "Mommy, Maggie, hurry up, let's go get in the cop car so I can turn on the siren!"

"Gary, Gary, calm down, you don't have to scream; we're right here," said Margaret. "You sound like a madman."

"Well, hurry up cuz I'm going to turn on the siren in the cop car. Officer Young said I could."

"No you can't," Margaret said. "Only the police are allowed to do that."

"Yes I can. Ask Mommy. She knows. Huh, Mommy?"

"Yes, honey, Officer Young said you could turn on the siren on the way home."

"Oh, wow!" Margaret gasped. "Can I do it too?"

"No, just me cuz you got hurt and you look like a zombie. And you're gonna be in the back seat so you can't reach the siren," said Little Gary.

It was approaching nine o'clock by the time they left the hospital. Margaret and her mother sat in the back seat, while Little Gary sat up front with Officer Young, anxiously waiting to turn on the siren. Sitting quietly with Margaret, his mother thought about her other five children. She wasn't worried because she knew they were being properly cared for by her neighbor, Mrs. Martinez, who was very close to the family. As for her husband, she hadn't talked to him since early that morning, just before he left the house to look for employment.

Once they were in the patrol car, Officer Young asked Little Gary if he was ready to push the siren button.

"Whoopee!" Little Gary yelled out. "Ah, ah, what do I do? What do I do?" he asked nervously.

"Just push this button on the dashboard," said Officer Young, "And—"

Little Gary immediately pushed down on the button causing the siren to make a loud blaring sound that startled him so much he jerked his hand back as if he had touched an electrical wire.

"Oooh-wee," Little Gary said, with his eyes opened wide as if he'd seen a ghost. "Mommy, Mommy, did you hear the loud sound I made? Did it scare you and Maggie?"

"Yes, Gary, I did hear it and it did scare us," his mother said.

"No, I didn't get scared," replied Margaret, sounding unconcerned.

"What happened, Little Cowboy? Why did you let go of the button so soon? It would have made different sounds. Do you want to do it again?" Officer Young asked.

"No, it, it got me scared," Gary said with a quiver in his voice.

The rest of the way home was solemn and quiet. Officer Young stared straight ahead into the evening lights, driving at a steady pace and thinking about his wife and three children waiting safely at home for his return. Margaret could be heard in the back seat talking softly to her mother about the accident, while Little Gary sat motionless in the front seat, gazing out the side window of the police car.

"Mother, I know what I did was wrong and I shouldn't have made Gary go with me to the store. He told me we shouldn't go, but I talked him into going anyway," Margaret confessed.

"Yes, it was wrong what you did. You should never have lied or disobeyed me. Nothing good ever comes out of lying. You should always be truthful, even if it means being scolded or not getting what you want. Just think, something really bad could have happened to you and Gary. Do you understand?"

"Yes, Mother, but it was that man's fault we got hit. We were being careful crossing the street and he just ran into us. He didn't even stop at the stop sign."

"Yes, honey, I was told that you looked both ways before you started to cross the street, but the point is you had no business being in the street in the first place. You should have been home playing outside in the front of the house, like I told you. The accident never would have happened if you had obeyed me. You have to learn to take responsibility for your actions. Do you understand what I'm saying?"

"Yes, but if—"

"No, Margaret, there are no buts or ifs about it. You were at fault, and you have to understand that. You can't be making excuses for your actions every time you do something wrong. You have to own up to the things you do and take responsibility. It is very important that you understand what I'm saying to you. Okay?"

"Yes, Mother, I understand."

"When Mrs. Martinez told me what happened, I was terrified. I thought the worst had happened to you and Gary. It was an awful feeling. However, I will say, I am very proud of you for protecting your brother the way you did. It was a very courageous act."

"What do you mean?" Margaret asked. "What are you talking about? What did I do?"

"Oh, sweetheart, you don't remember, do you?"

"No, what did I do?"

"Just before the truck hit you, you pushed Gary out of the way so he wouldn't get hit. That's what you did. And it was very brave of you to do that. It showed that you thought more of his safety than your own."

"Well, I don't remember doing that. I don't even remember getting hit by the truck. All that I remember is being in the ambulance."

Just as Margaret uttered her last words, she snuggled up closer to her mother, gently placed her head on her mother's lap, and closed her eyes. At that moment, a peacefulness enveloped Mrs. Trujillo as she held her precious daughter ever so lightly in her arms.

Still awake in the front seat, sounds of oohs and ahs were heard coming from Little Gary, as he looked out the window of the police car at all the city lights, wishing he still clutched in his hands the brown bag of candy corn he and his sister had bought earlier that day, which ended up scattered all over the street in front of Straight's Grocery Store.

Gee, he thought, as he rubbed his sleepy eyes, *I didn't even get to eat any of my candy corn.*

Hostess CupCake
chapter two

He found it especially hard to sleep one cold night in December, tossing and turning all night long in the rollaway bed he shared with his three younger brothers. All Little Gary could think of this wintery night was eating lunch at school the next day, an event that seldom occurred since his family was extremely poor and could not afford daily sack lunches for the five school-age children. Taking a sack lunch to school was considered a treat because going home for lunch usually meant eating leftovers from the night before, sometimes *caldito* (broth with fried potatoes and ground beef) or tortillas and beans. This time, however, Little Gary was going to carry a sack lunch to school consisting of a bologna sandwich, banana, and a Hostess CupCake. It was his mother's way of rewarding him for seeing to it that there was a sufficient supply of wood and coal for cooking and heating.

The neighborhood kids walking to school with Little Gary the next morning would be green with envy since they too were just as poor and would have to go home for lunch and most likely eat leftovers from the night before.

As morning came, Little Gary crawled quietly out of bed, careful not to wake up his brothers and his three older sisters who slept only inches away on another rollaway bed. Little Gary was up much earlier this school day than on other days. He wanted to make sure his lunch was still in the icebox, especially the Hostess CupCake he couldn't stop thinking about all night.

As he tiptoed into the kitchen toward the icebox, he gently placed his hand on the door handle and opened it slowly. And as the door swung open a thought occurred to him: *What if it's gone? What if someone took my Hostess CupCake? What will I tell Johnny and Leonard?* After all, it was only yesterday when Little Gary had bragged to his friends about taking lunch to school, which usually meant a special treat. But nothing to worry about: there, next to the banana and on top of the bologna sandwich was the very thing Little Gary had lost sleep over, the twin-size cupcakes tightly wrapped in cellophane.

A short time later, the rest of the family began waking up to start their day. The other children were not as fortunate as Little Gary; for them it meant walking home during the lunch hour and eating leftovers from the night before, most likely gravy and potatoes. As they got dressed, folded up the rollaway beds and straightened up around the living room, where they all slept, Little Gary was happily picking up after himself and quietly humming his favorite tune, "Hey Baba Reba," which he often hummed or sang whenever he was excited or nervous.

Shortly after, his mother called from the kitchen: "Gary, come and eat your breakfast. I don't want you running off to school without eating like you did yesterday," she scolded.

Without saying anything Little Gary sat down at the kitchen table, poured milk into a bowl of oatmeal mixed with cornflakes that his mother had prepared for him, and began to eat.

"Did you pick up your clothes from the floor like I asked you?"

"Yes, Mother," Little Gary answered while inhaling and slurping his cereal.

"Make sure you come straight home from school today." His mother continued talking to him as he ate his breakfast. "You need to chop some more wood for tonight; it's going to be very cold and it might even snow. Okay?"

"Yes, Mom, I will," he answered with his mouth half full of milk, now rolling down his chin.

It was Little Gary's responsibility to make sure there was plenty of wood chopped up in small pieces to fit in both the woodstove in the kitchen used for cooking and the potbellied stove used for providing heat in the living room, where all seven children slept. The bedroom where Little Gary's parents slept was warmed only by whatever heat flowed under the bedroom door from both stoves.

After eating breakfast, Little Gary grabbed his sack lunch from the icebox and checked once more to see if his Hostess CupCake was still in the bag. With a smile on his face, he grabbed his coat from the chair, walked over to his mother and kissed her on the cheek. Then he left through the back door, where he was joined by his friends Roy, Johnny, and Leonard.

"Damn, Garr, it's about time you came out," Johnny said, shivering.

"Yeah, man, we're freezing our *huevos* off," said Leonard.

"What *huevos*? You ain't got any. All you got are 'peas,' and little ones," Roy said to Leonard as he and Johnny laughed. "Isn't that right, Gary?"

"Why don't you guys lay off Leonard; you know he's self-conscious about his little 'peas,'" Little Gary joined in as they all laughed at Leonard's expense.

"Yeah, Garr, how come it takes you so long to get ready for school?" Johnny asked.

"I had to eat breakfast. My mom got mad cuz I didn't eat yesterday before I went to school," Little Gary explained.

"*Pobrecito* Gary, his mommy made him eat breakfast. What was it you ate, *frijoles*?" his friends teased.

"Okay, okay, let's go. Enough," said Little Gary.

As the four friends left for school they were joined by several other neighborhood kids. As always, whenever they were all bunched together, they playfully pushed and punched one another. This day, however, Little Gary was not in such a playful mood; rather, he was preoccupied while walking quietly along with his friends, swinging his lunch bag back and forth. With every stride in his walk, he was smiling and enjoying the camaraderie with his friends while composing himself with the excitement of taking lunch to school. Of course the other kids couldn't let him escape the horseplay. He, too, had to be included in all the roughhousing. For starters, his friends just had to know why Little Gary was so happy and what was in the bag he was carrying.

"Whatcha got there, Garr?" asked Felix.

"Yeah, Garr, whatcha got in the bag?" Leroy shouted out.

"Come on, Garr, tell 'em whatcha got in the bag," Johnny and Leonard said together since they both knew he was taking lunch to school, after all the bragging he had done the day before.

"Don't tell us your mommy made you a sack lunch so you don't have to walk home at lunchtime with us *pobres*. What did she make you, a burrito or a potato sandwich?" teased Leroy, which brought laughter from the other kids.

"Why don't you split it with us?" Arthur said.

"Yeah," the other kids joined in.

"Then when your mommy asks why you came home for lunch, just tell her the birds ate it," continued Arthur.

"It's not a burrito, Leroy," Little Gary said. "And there's no way I'm sharing my lunch with you guys. Take your own lunch."

"We would have, but we don't have anything to eat 'cept beans and tortillas," someone said on behalf of the group, "And no way we're bringing that to school or everybody will laugh at us."

Little Gary and his friends were always teasing and making fun of one another. It was a game they played and each had turns being picked on. Except, of course, for Roy, who was a year older than most of the kids in the neighborhood, due to being held back a year in school. Roy didn't take kidding very well, but he sure could dish it out.

Once they'd arrived at school, the kids scattered all over the schoolyard to get in a few minutes of playing time before the school bell rang. Instead of joining his friends as they played marbles, wrestled on the ground, kicked dirt on each other, and pulled the girls' ponytails, Little Gary stood near the school entrance, up against the wall, clutching his lunch bag and waiting for the bell. He didn't want to let go of his lunch bag for fear of losing it.

Minutes later, a loud piercing noise blasted out over the school grounds, invoking sounds of disappointment from the children. "Damn," "Shit," or "Darn," could be heard throughout the schoolyard as the children ran toward the school entrance. Little Gary was already inside the building ahead of the other kids. He ran to his hall locker to put away his coat and lunch bag, while fantasizing about the Hostess CupCake he was going to have with lunch.

Once the students were in class the school bell rang a second time, which meant that all the children had to be seated at their desks. Without exception though, Rudy, the self-imposed teacher's aide, was always the last person to take his seat. He would wait until all the other kids were seated and then he would walk in, dragging his feet and telling everyone to be quiet. If he saw someone not yet seated, he would shout: "Didn't you hear the bell or are you deaf?" And each time the children would all yell at him to settle down and be quiet: he wasn't in charge; the teacher was.

"All right class, everyone settle down," Miss Tiger, the second-grade teacher calmly said. "It's time for the Pledge of Allegiance, so everyone please rise and place your right hand over your heart. I want to hear it said loud and clear. Okay?"

As the thirty or so children stood up, you could hear giggling, sliding chairs, pencils dropping on the floor, and shushing noises by some of the kids.

"I pledge of the allegiance to the flag of the United States of America for which it stands on one individual and on top of God, for liberty, justice, and the suit of happiness."

"All right children, it seems we have a lot of work to do in reciting allegiance to our flag."

Though the children were still having difficulties reciting the Pledge of Allegiance, it was the sound of innocence in their voices that warmed Miss Tiger's heart—the very reason she became a teacher. She loved every minute she spent with the children. It was her second year at Federal Elementary; for four years she'd been teaching grade school.

After graduating college at the top of her class, Miss Tiger was placed in an upper-middle-class elementary school for the gifted. But after only two years teaching there, she transferred to Federal Elementary. As a gifted person herself, she was not content nor fulfilled teaching the best and the brightest in an environment surrounded by wealth and privilege.

Although Miss Tiger loved her students dearly, her heart had not been in her work. Teaching at Emerald

Heights Academy, she felt, was like merely polishing diamonds when she wanted to be carving out jewels. So, despite how family and friends felt about her leaving such a prestigious school, not to mention the potential career opportunities, she transferred to Federal Elementary, the poorest school in the district, to teach children whose futures seemed bleak at best but whose demeanors still radiated with spirit much like those of the children at Emerald Heights. Not only did she transfer to the district's most underfunded elementary school, she spent a good part of her time participating in after-school and community events.

"Okay, children, settle down and please be seated," Miss Tiger uttered with a lump in her throat. "Now, who can tell me where we left off yesterday?"

No sooner had she asked the question than Little Gary raised his hand, which was somewhat unusual since he never volunteered to participate in class. He always seemed a little shy when it came to talking in front of the other children, and it didn't help that his friend Roy teased everyone who was called on to speak in front of the class. Only this time, Little Gary paid no attention to Roy's teasing since he was too excited and anxious about what was waiting for him in his locker.

"Yes, Gary," Miss Tiger acknowledged.

"We were learning the times table."

"That's right, Gary, thank you. Now, who could tell me what five times five is?" Miss Tiger continued.

Again, without hesitation, Little Gary's arm shot straight up.

"Thanks, Gary, but I want to hear from someone else

this time." *My, what has gotten into Gary, I've never seen him this excited,* Miss Tiger thought to herself.

"Twenty-five," yelled out Gloria.

"That's the correct answer," Miss Tiger said. "But next time, raise your hand and wait to be called on. Okay?"

"Yes, Miss Tiger," Gloria said respectfully.

As time drew closer to the noon hour, Little Gary sat excitedly at his desk with his arms folded, looking around the classroom, and sort of humming an unfamiliar tune while at the same time daydreaming about the cream-filled cupcakes his mother had packed away in his lunch bag, never mind the bologna sandwich and banana, since it wasn't every day a treat like this came along.

As his mind wandered back to the commotions in the classroom, Little Gary could hear Miss Tiger from a distance instructing the children to take out their reading books.

"It's your turn to read, Roy," Miss Tiger said. "Please turn to page thirteen. I want the rest of the class to follow along because I will be calling on someone else to read next, so please pay attention. Okay, Roy, you may begin."

As Roy stood up to read, his face turned bright red with embarrassment, not that the other children would laugh or make fun of him, but because he hated to read out loud in front of all the other students. Besides, Roy was considered the strongest second grader in class and even stronger than many of the third graders, so no one dared laugh or make fun of him or they were in for it after school. Roy was always roughhousing in the schoolyard, challenging the other boys in a whistling match, which almost always ended up in a fistfight.

Before opening his mouth to begin reading, Roy glanced over at Little Gary for some sort of support since he and Little Gary were the best of friends and he could always count on him for a sign of encouragement. This time, however, Little Gary didn't acknowledge Roy, as he sat at his desk, erect, arms folded, feet dangling, smiling from ear to ear, and staring at the wall clock, patiently waiting for the noon bell to ring.

When Roy finished reading, he again looked over at Little Gary, who this time gave Roy a quick glance with a smile and a thumbs-up.

While listening to the children read, Miss Tiger sat at her desk and gazed over the sea of little minds, thinking how much she loved teaching at Federal Elementary. *I am so happy teaching here; I wouldn't have it any other way,* she thought to herself.

By the time the noon hour approached, the children were raring to jump out of their seats and head home for lunch, but first they had to hear the sound Little Gary had been waiting for since arriving at school that morning and which was music to his ears that special day.

As the bell sounded and the other kids were scrambling around, stuffing their papers, pencils, and books inside the top of their desks, Little Gary was all set to go.

"All right, children, settle down," Miss Tiger instructed. "No one is going anywhere until everyone is sitting quietly in their seat."

"Roy, keep your hands to yourself," Miss Tiger scolded.

"But she started it," he answered.

"No I didn't, you troublemaker," Gloria said.

"Come on, Roy: cool it, knock it off," chided Little Gary. Little Gary was the only one of Roy's friends who could stand up to him without being pounced on.

"Okay, now quietly get up from your seat and form a single line behind Gary," Miss Tiger calmly instructed the kids. "Okay, Gary, you may lead the class out. Have a good lunch and I'll see you all back here in forty-five minutes," she lovingly told the children as they scurried off down the hallway and out the front door.

While most of Little Gary's classmates went home for lunch, he remained in the hallway a few minutes, feeling somewhat uncomfortable since this was his first time eating lunch at school. He felt all alone. Trying to compose himself, he began slowly walking toward the wall lockers to get his sack lunch before heading to the school gymnasium, where he would be having his lunch since the school's lunchroom was still under repair because of broken water pipes. His pace quickened as he felt a little more confident. He didn't dare run for fear of being reported by the hall monitor, Mr. Otto, also the gym teacher, who had hall monitor duty three days a week. Keeping his brisk stride, he passed Mr. Otto, and looking up at him with a big smile, said, "Afternoon, Mr. Otto."

"Good afternoon, Gary. Where you headed? Aren't you going home for lunch today?" he asked.

"Oh no," Little Gary responded. "I brang my lunch to school today, and guess what? I have a Hostess CupCake in my lunch bag."

"You do, huh?" replied Mr. Otto. "Well, don't eat it too fast. I don't want you to get sick this afternoon in gym class; we're going to play Elimination."

"Oh, wow! That's my favorite game," said Little Gary as he strode even faster toward the wall lockers.

Reaching his wall locker, while humming "Hey Baba Reba," Little Gary fumbled with the locker door latch until it opened. There, at the bottom of the locker, between a "Big Chief" writing tablet and a box of crayons, was the brown paper lunch bag he'd protectively held on to on his way to school only hours earlier as he fought off his friends from trying to coax him into sharing his lunch with them.

As he reached in to pick up his lunch bag, the same thought he had earlier that morning entered his mind: *Is it still there?* Then, once in his hand, something felt different, causing his stomach to turn. He noticed the lunch bag was lighter than it was when carrying it to school that morning. Taking a deep breath, he slowly unfolded the bag, looked inside and was suddenly overcome with emotion. It was gone. The one thing most on his mind since the day before was gone. He could not believe it! His Hostess CupCake was gone.

So devastated and stunned, and not fully conscious of his actions, Little Gary leaned up against the wall lockers with his head titled back, looking up toward the ceiling, as if asking why, while his small body frame slowly slid down to the floor. His head gently fell into his hands, which were resting on his knees, and he began to cry.

Minutes later, Miss Tiger was on her way to the teachers' lounge when she saw someone sitting on the floor against the wall lockers. "Is that you, Gary?" she asked. But there was no response from the rolled-up little figure against the wall lockers. "Gary?" Miss Tiger asked again.

With a crackling in his voice and sounds of sniffling, without looking up, Little Gary said quietly, "Uh, uh, uh-huh."

"What's wrong, Gary?" Miss Tiger asked with much emotion and concern in her voice.

Slowly lifting up his head, with tears rolling down his cheeks and the sound of heartbreak in his voice, Little Gary murmured softly, "Sum . . . sum . . . somebody . . . took my . . . my . . . Hostess CupCake I . . . I . . . brang for lunch and I . . . I . . . really, really wanted it."

Sobbing much heavily now, Little Gary lowered his head back into his hands as Miss Tiger sat down on the floor beside him and gently placed her arm around his little shoulders to console him. Seconds later the warmth of her touch generated a soothing effect in Little Gary's throbbing heart, causing the quivering of his small body to gradually subside.

Trying to think of something to say to Little Gary to ease his pain while at the same time instill in his mind something of value rather than merely appease him, Miss Tiger, in a soft, gentle tone, said, "You know, Gary, sometimes things happen to us that may cause a lot of pain and sorrow, and although it hurts a lot, we have to learn to accept it because we need to become strong. That's how life is, Gary: sometimes happy things happen to us and sometimes sad things happen to us. Do you understand what I'm saying, Gary?"

With a nod of his head, Little Gary, still curled up on the floor and overwhelmed by what happened, whispered, "I . . . I . . . think so, but, but I rea-really wanted to eat my Hostess CupCake."

"I know you did, Gary, and I know how badly you must feel right now, but you will get over it because you are a strong little boy. Come on, let's go to the gymnasium so you can eat your lunch. The afternoon bell is going to ring in a few minutes and you need to get something in your little tummy so your stomach doesn't growl in class; you might scare the other kids."

Lifting his head up, while wiping his eyes with his shirtsleeve and trying to put a smile on his face, Little Gary said, "Oh, Miss Tiger, they can't hear my stomach."

"Well, maybe not, but you can't learn anything with an empty stomach, so let's go eat lunch because I'm hungry too," Miss Tiger said, then smiled as she raised herself up from the floor and reached down to help Little Gary to his feet.

They then walked, hand in hand, down the hallway and through the swinging doors toward the gymnasium. As they reached the entrance, Miss Tiger looked down at Little Gary and said, "Remember, you are a strong little boy and what happened to you will only make you stronger. I'll see you in class after lunch, okay?"

Shaking his head yes, their hands parted and Miss Tiger walked slowly away while slightly turning around to see him still standing there at the entrance as though he was contemplating whether to go in. He just stood there.

After a moment's thought, Little Gary wiped his eyes again with his shirtsleeve, held his head up high, pushed open the gymnasium doors, and proudly walked inside.

Beans

chapter three

Snow had just started falling when Little Gary and his friends, Roy, Johnny, and Leonard, left the school grounds to go home. It was the last day of school before Christmas break—excitement filled the air. Children ran in all different directions, throwing snowballs and chasing after one another. Even some of the teachers took part in the frolic that December day.

Walking home along the highway, Little Gary and his friends threw snowballs at passing cars and trucks, then prepared to take off running just in case one of the drivers made a sudden stop and chased after them. They did not want a repeat occurrence of what had happened to Roy on another occasion.

Roy had been chased down by a truck driver, who grabbed him by the collar and flung him into the bushes as if he were a rag doll. The truck driver then looked around for the other boys, who by that time were nowhere to be found. After that day, Roy vowed never to be caught again. The other boys, of course, thought the incident was funny and laughed all the way home, running as fast as their feet could carry them.

Throwing snowballs at passing vehicles was a contest to see who could hit the most cars, trucks, or buses. Roy, Johnny, and Leonard seemed to always enjoy the thrill and excitement of doing something that was somewhat dangerous. As for Little Gary, he was more cautious not to do something that could get him into trouble. So when it came to this particular activity, Little Gary knew it was not only dangerous but also wrong. So when his friends were having the time of their lives competing to see who could hit the most vehicles, Little Gary didn't really put much effort into trying to hit his target. His friends, of course, would tease him and say he threw like a little girl—though the teasing didn't bother him. What really concerned Little Gary was the thought of his father finding out what he had been doing and sending him to bed without dinner, but first with a few whacks on his behind with a strap, and this day could not be one of those times.

For on this particular day his mother was making his favorite food: beans. Little Gary loved eating beans. He would rather eat beans than any other sort of food. Even if he had a choice between eating a Hostess CupCake, which he ate on rare occasions, or beans, he would most definitely choose beans. So he had to be very careful not to get into any more trouble that would cause him to be punished by his father, since it was only a few weeks earlier that his father sent him to bed without dinner for giving his friends each a slice of bologna. Nevertheless, later that evening his older sister, Lucinda, saw to it he didn't fall asleep hungry and fixed him a plate of food.

Little Gary's mother had just bought groceries that unforgettable day and it had seemed okay to him to share some bologna with his friends. What Little Gary didn't know, however, was that his father had counted the slices of bologna for rationing purposes since there were nine family members in the household and food was in short supply.

Sharing food with one another was a common thing between Little Gary and his friends, so it never really occurred to him that his father would get upset. He thought maybe it had something to do with the fact that his father had just recently lost his job again and was merely releasing some of his frustration.

Throwing snowballs at passing vehicles that snowy afternoon turned into chasing after the girls and targeting them instead.

"Hey, you guys, stop that," yelled Gloria. "I'm going to tell my brother and he's going to kick your butt," she said as she brushed snow off her head.

"Go get your brother; we'll nail him with snowballs too," Roy said.

"Yeah, go get your brother," echoed Johnny and Leonard, "we'll kick his ass."

"Hey, you guys, come on, let's split. Have you seen her brother? He's in the sixth grade and he's pretty bad," cautioned Little Gary.

"So?" Leonard said. "There are four of us and we're pretty bad too."

"What's the matter, Garr, you scared?" Johnny asked. "Maybe we should kick your ass."

"Yeah, well go ahead and try," Little Gary boldly said.

The four boys had been friends since before kindergarten and could tease one another and even get into fights and still remain friends. Their bond was tight and their loyalty strong. For fun they would wrestle on the unpaved dirt streets to test their might, climb billboards as a display of courage, and walk the train tracks to see who could go the farthest without falling off. At times they would even walk the rails on the viaduct, which was a very dangerous thing to do.

Now in the fourth grade they had a reputation at school and in their neighborhood because of their roughhousing antics. Among the four boys, Roy was considered the strongest and roughest kid in the neighborhood, perhaps because he was held back in school and a year older than his friends.

Little Gary was next in age, and though small in stature, he never flaunted his physical attributes or displayed any meanness with the other kids the way Roy did. Johnny, who was a few inches taller and heavier than his three friends, was also somewhat of a bully like Roy but not as boisterous. Leonard on the other hand was slender and somewhat frail looking; he simply followed along with whatever his friends did.

Their neighborhood was a depressed low-income area near the inner city, partly residential and partly industrial. The streets were unpaved, and weeds filled the vacant lots where they played War and Cowboys and Indians.

Little Gary, Johnny, and Leonard lived in a two-story house, which was converted into three separate family dwellings. Johnny lived upstairs with his mother, older sister, younger brother, an aunt, and grandparents. Little Gary and Leonard lived on the ground level in two dwellings separated by a paper-thin wall. Leonard lived with his mother, three brothers, a sister, a cousin, and an uncle. Little Gary lived with both of his parents, three older sisters, and three younger brothers. In all, twenty-four people lived in a two-story nine-room house heated by woodstoves, and they shared an outside toilet located inside a coal bin. Years later, the house that the three friends lived in was considered unsuitable living conditions and was condemned by the city.

Roy, on the other hand, lived across the street with his grandparents in a two-bedroom house with a large fenced-in yard. No one ever knew why Roy didn't live with his parents and his three younger siblings, who lived on the other side of town, and it never occurred to anyone to ask.

The younger kids in the neighborhood all attended the same elementary school, which was on the other side of a river and across a busy two-lane highway, though it wasn't very far. The older kids, junior high and high school age, had to travel across town to attend school, which was considerably farther away and required crossing over a viaduct that extended over a train yard.

Arriving home from school that snowy afternoon after throwing snowballs at moving vehicles without getting caught, and ambushing the girls, Little Gary and his friends agreed to meet later that evening in Roy's backyard to talk about their plans for the Christmas holiday. On most holidays and weekends Little Gary and his friends sold newspapers in the downtown area as a way of making a little spending money. And on game night at the baseball stadium they sold the *Saturday Evening Post*, which was exciting for them since they not only earned a few dollars but also were able to see the Denver Bears play for free. Then, once the baseball game ended, they were driven home in the newspaper van around the midnight hour.

"Later, man," Roy said as he jumped over the fence and walked toward the back door of his house.

"Later," the other boys said.

"Where have you been, Gary?" his mother asked. "Margaret and Paulie were home an hour ago. They said school let out early today because of Christmas break."

"We-we stayed in the schoolyard and had a snowball fight," he answered while looking down at the floor, something he did when he wasn't completely truthful.

"Well, you know you're supposed to chop some wood before your dad comes home."

"Yes, Mom, I know. Are we still having beans for supper?"

"We will if you hurry and go chop some wood and bring in some coal. Otherwise, we'll have sandwiches," his mother said jokingly.

"Okay! Okay!" Little Gary said excitedly and ran out the back door into the garage, where the wood was stored near a cesspool, though it was securely covered for safety reasons.

The coal bin housing the toilet was next to the garage, though there was a partition separating the two.

As Little Gary opened the door to the toilet to enter the coal bin, he heard a voice yell out, "Hey, shut that f---'n door; can't you see I'm in here?" It was Victor, his next-door neighbor, Leonard's older brother, who startled Little Gary.

"Can't you wait until I'm finished crap'n? You little fart."

"Well, you didn't lock the door," Little Gary snapped back.

"What do you mean 'lock,' there's no f---'n lock to this shithouse. Anyway, you're going to have to wait till I'm finished crapping, so get the hell out of here."

To avoid any further verbal abuse from Leonard's older brother, Little Gary left without uttering another word.

Meanwhile, he went back to the garage, where the woodpile was, picked up his ax and began chopping wood. He was happy about having beans for supper that evening and began singing, "Beans, beans, the magical fruit, the more you eat, the more you toot." After happily singing several verses of the rhyming song, he realized he had chopped a large pile of wood, so he stacked it neatly near the back door. He then checked the toilet again, and seeing that it was now unoccupied, went inside to fill the coal bucket. Next he gathered up several pieces of wood, while still holding on to the coal bucket, and carefully opened the screen door with one hand. He used his foot to keep the screen door from closing, then reached in to turn the doorknob and push open the door with his knee.

"Here, Gary, let me help," his mother said as she reached for the coal bucket.

"No, no, I wanna do this," Little Gary said, wobbling over toward the kitchen stove and gently setting down the coal bucket and armload of wood. "Well, I'm all finished," he said to his mother as he wiped his hands on his pant legs. "When we gonna eat?"

"You mean, 'When are we going to eat?'" his mother corrected him.

"Yeah, that's what I mean," retorted Little Gary, but in a friendly way.

"Not until around six o'clock," his mother said. "Besides, I still have to put the beans on and let them cook for a few hours, or do you want to eat them raw?" his mother said kiddingly. "But if you help, maybe we could eat earlier."

"How earlier?" Little Gary asked.

"Maybe five thirty or so. Besides it's still early and Cindy and Frances haven't come home from school and your father is not home yet. So if you want to help, you can clean the beans for me and put them in the pan that's on the stove, then fill the pan with water. I'll get the fire going. Okay, *mijo*?"

"Okay, I'll do it."

It was his mother's day off from work, which made it even more special for him. He loved having his mother home, even if he was outside all day playing and didn't see her; just knowing she was home made him feel secure and all warm inside.

Little Gary's mother worked the swing shift at the hospital as a nurse aide and only saw her children in the mornings and on her days off. A neighbor, Mrs. Benavidez babysat the twins, Daniel and Donald, until Margaret, the youngest daughter, returned home from school with Paulie. Then Cindy and Frances, once they got home from school, would share in the responsibilities of caring for the family, which included preparing dinner, tending to house chores, and seeing to it that all went well during the rest of the evening hours.

Friday nights when Little Gary didn't have to go to bed early, he and his friends would walk over the viaduct to meet his mother when she got off the bus after working from early afternoon to midnight. On some nights his father would walk across the viaduct and escort his wife safely home. Usually his mother would end up walking home alone, though she never seemed to worry about her safety.

On other occasions when Little Gary was instructed by his older sister to stay in the front yard, he would sit on the fence and count the cars as they drove by, wishing at any minute his mother would be dropped off, knowing of course that would never happen.

The nights were long and the work was hard, but what his mother loved most about her work at the hospital was caring for the elderly. She would often say of the aged, "If we accept our old people with kindness and compassion, God will lighten the load." Little Gary's mother had been the family's sole provider since his father could not maintain steady employment due to his drinking.

"Mom, I finished cleaning the beans and I put them in the water."

"Okay, honey, you may go outside now until it's time to eat," she said as she stood at the table, making the tortilla dough.

Little Gary loved the smell of tortillas and beans. Every day when he came home from school, the first thing he would do was open the icebox door to see if his mother had made beans before leaving for work, and if she had, his face would immediately light up. But if she hadn't, he would feel disappointed.

"Say, Garr, wanna play marbles?" Leonard asked.

"Play marbles? What, you crazy? Can't you see there's snow on the ground, or are you blind too?"

"Come on, we can clean off a spot and play."

"Nah, I don't think so."

"Then let's go in the back and have a snowball fight."

"Okay. But I can't play too long cuz I'm gonna have to go eat supper. We're having beans."

"Damn, Garr, is that all you guys eat? You do know what they say about beans, don't you?"

"Yeah, yeah, I know: 'Beans, beans, the magical fruit, the more Leonard eats, the more Leonard toots.'"

"Heck," Leonard said, "I can toot eating cornflakes."

"What are you guys gonna eat?" Little Gary asked.

"I don't know," Leonard said. "Maybe spaghetti or macaroni. That's what Victor likes. He can't seem to get enough. Just like you and your beans, I guess."

"Speaking of your brother, he just about bit my head off."

"What do you mean, Garr?"

"I was getting coal from the coal bin, and he happened to be taking a dump, so I guess I interrupted him."

"Yeah I know, he's a prick. But don't tell him or he'll kick my ass."

Food always seemed to be the topic of conversation between Little Gary and Leonard. On occasion both families would share a Sunday evening dinner; that is, if Gary's mother didn't have to work.

The two families lived next to each other, separated by a doorway locked with an oversized safety pin. So when dinner plans were made to share their resources, the safety pin was removed and the door was opened to conveniently maneuver back and forth.

"Macaroni, huh? We had that last night," Little Gary said. "But I still would rather eat beans."

"Well, are we gonna have a snowball fight or spend the rest of the day talking about beans?" asked Leonard.

Just then Little Gary surprised Leonard by stuffing snow down his back.

"Hey, man, cool it," Leonard said, shivering and jumping up and down, trying to remove the snow from under his shirt and pulling it from out of his pants.

"Say, I got an idea," Little Gary said. "Instead of getting all wet with snow, let's go get Roy and Johnny and go see if Officer Young is under the viaduct with his motorcycle, waiting to chase speeders."

"Hey, yeah, let's go," Leonard said excitedly. "But Johnny isn't home. I saw him taking off earlier. Besides, I thought you had to go eat your beans."

"Yeah, I do, but it's not time yet. Come on, let's go."

As the two friends walked across the street to Roy's house, Little Gary suggested they clobber him with snowballs when he came outside. But Leonard responded, "Heck no! The last time I hit him with a snowball he kicked my ass, so I'm not doing that again, so forget it."

"Come on, don't be *skamau*, you chicken," said Little Gary.

"You do it," Leonard said, "and see what he does to you."

"Okay, I will, but you call him and I'll wait on the side of the house so when he comes out, I'll nail him."

"Are you sure you want to do this?" Leonard said, still shaken by the thought.

"Sure, why not, he's always screwing with us, isn't he? Remember the time he put mud in our shoes when we went swimming in the Platte River? He thought that was pretty funny, didn't he? Well, I didn't think it was so funny and neither did my dad, cuz he got really mad at me when he saw my shoes on the back porch all wet and muddy."

"Yeah, but Roy can't take a joke like we can."

"What do you mean 'like we can'? It's no joke when your old man yells at you and puts you to bed without dinner. Come on, do you want in or not?" Little Gary said with a scolding sound in his voice.

"Okay, okay, I'll do it," Leonard said as he walked up to the back door of Roy's house. "But don't get carried away with the snowballs. Okay?"

"All right, I won't. Hurry up and let's get this over with so we can go see Officer Young before he splits for home. Be-besides, I have to go home and eat my *frijoles*."

Just as Leonard approached Roy's back porch, the door suddenly opened wide and a loud voice yelled out, *"Qué quieres, muchacho?"*

At that moment Leonard was so startled that he fell backward off the two-foot-high porch, landing softly on a freshly covered blanket of snow.

"Is, is Roy home?" Leonard asked, looking up at a giant of a man.

"No, Roy *no está aquí. Quítate*," Roy's grandpa loudly

snapped at Leonard, who then jumped to his feet as he and Little Gary took off running.

"Damn, that old man is mean," Leonard said as he tried to catch his breath. "He scared the shit out of me. I didn't expect to see him."

"He is a grumpy old fart, isn't he?" said Little Gary as he, too, was breathing heavily.

When the boys reached the viaduct, Officer Young was not there.

"Damn, we missed him," Leonard said. "I hope he comes back."

"He will," said Little Gary. "He's probably chasing a speeder."

Visiting with Officer Young was always an exciting moment for the neighborhood kids. Every day after school, and sometimes on weekends, they would gather around him under the viaduct, where he stationed himself out of view of the motorists, while telling them stories of his many car chases and motorcycle accidents, which sometimes landed him in the hospital.

He was the police officer who had waited patiently at the hospital while Little Gary and his sister Margaret were being examined after the candy corn accident and then he drove them home, along with their mother. Though Little Gary didn't quite remember the details of the accident, he led his friends to believe that he and his sister were saved by Officer Young. Which of course his friends teased him about.

"See, what I tell you, here comes Officer Young," Little Gary said to Leonard.

"Hi, Officer Young," the boys yelled out.

"Hi there, guys. How goes it?" Officer Young yelled back over the roar of his motorcycle as he came to a stop.

"What are you kids doing here, standing in the cold? Shouldn't you be home where it's all warm and cozy?"

"Nah, we'd rather be here, watching you chase speeders. How many did you catch this time?" Little Gary asked.

"Oh, about three. It's been a pretty safe day and that's good. The less I have to chase, the better I like it."

Just then another motorist came racing down the viaduct, causing Officer Young to instinctively kick-start his motorcycle, and within seconds he was off chasing the speeding vehicle until it came to a complete stop a few blocks away.

"Wow, he's fast," a voice yelled out from down the street.

"Hey, it's Johnny and Roy," Leonard called out to their friends, who were mesmerized by the sight of Officer Young in action.

"Where you guys been?" Leonard asked. "Garr and I went to your house, Roy, but your grandpa ran us off; said you weren't home."

"I was home, but I was in the can, and my gramps didn't know."

"What were you doing, smoking another one of your grandma's cigs?" Little Gary asked.

"No, but I did sneak a whole pack this time, so we could light up tonight. Oh, I forgot, you don't smoke; you're all *skamau* you're gonna get caught," Roy said, teasing Little Gary.

Roy had a habit of taking cigarettes from his grandma's apron pocket and going into the bathroom to smoke, thinking all the time no one would find out what he was up to.

"I'm not afraid, you butthead. I just don't wanna get all smelly from the smoke."

"Yeah, we know," said Johnny in a disbelieving tone.

"Say, you guys, I have to go home. I'll see you later after I eat supper," Little Gary said.

"We'll be over at my pad," replied Roy.

"See you later, Garr," the guys said.

"There he goes again," Little Gary said, referring to Officer Young, as he walked away.

As Little Gary opened the front door to his house, the aroma of freshly cooked beans filled the air. He could hardly wait to eat his beans and tortillas. He had also hoped they were having fried potatoes for dinner. He loved fried potatoes with beans. Sometimes his mother would also make Spanish rice, another favorite.

"Is that you, Gary?" his mother called out from the kitchen.

"Yes, Mom. Is it time to eat?"

"Not quite," his mother responded. "Your father isn't here yet."

"Do we have to wait for him? I'm starving. He's probably at the Frog Hollow, drinking with his buddies."

"Well, if he doesn't come home soon, we'll eat without him."

"I don't know if I can wait that long; I'm so hungry," Little Gary said, holding on to his stomach.

"You're always hungry. Now go out and bring in some

more wood for the stove, but first, go upstairs and call the girls so that they can set the table."

Little Gary didn't waste any time as he ran out the back door and up the outside staircase, calling out to his sisters, who were visiting with Johnny's older sister, Val, to come and eat.

Again Little Gary called out to his sisters, "Cindy, Frances, Maggie, come and eat now. Mother wants you to come and set the table, so hurry up."

Then, running back down the stairs, he quickly gathered an armload of firewood and went into the house.

As Little Gary was putting a couple of pieces of wood into the stove, he called out to his mother several times, but she didn't answer, so he sat down at the kitchen table, where a steaming hot bowl of beans sat. Although he was ready to eat at that moment, he thought maybe he should wait a few minutes until the rest of the family showed up. After waiting, no one else showed up so he decided to eat without them.

Sitting there at the table by himself, it occurred to him, again, that maybe he should wait since it seemed strange that no one else was there to eat with him. The girls were still upstairs and his mother had disappeared, along with Paulie and the twins. As for his father, it was pretty common for him not to come home until late in the evening, drunk.

So Little Gary decided to eat without the rest of the family. Sitting on a wooden bench and leaning forward, he carefully lifted a spoon of hot beans and blew softly so as not to spray bean juice all over the table. As he ate quietly alone, he could only think of how much he enjoyed eating beans.

Still, after several more minutes passed, no one had yet come to eat dinner so he continued eating until the bowl of beans was empty. Then just as he finished, his mother walked into the kitchen with the twins at her side and Paulie following behind.

"Gary, where are the girls? Did you call them?"

"Yes I did, but they didn't want to come, then when I came back you weren't here either, so I waited and waited and you guys still didn't come, so I ate the bowl of beans you set on the table for me."

"Gary," his mother said with a surprised look on her face and a concerned tone in her voice, "you did what?"

"I ate the bowl of beans you set on the table for me."

"Gary, the bowl of beans was a serving bowl. It wasn't meant just for you. I had just set the bowl down on the table when Mrs. Benavidez knocked on the wall and asked me to come over. She needed to see me about something. So that's where I was."

"Well . . . well, I waited and no one came and I was hungry, so I ate them. I didn't know they were for everybody. It looked like a small bowl, and I thought you served them for me cuz I told you I was really hungry."

Just then the girls all rushed in through the back door, screaming they were hungry and ready to eat, when Paulie yelled out, "We don't have anything to eat anymore cuz Gary ate all the beans in the bowl and now they're all gone."

"What?" Cindy asked loudly. "How could he eat all the beans?"

"Yeah," Frances blurted out. "Gary couldn't have eaten

all the beans; there's too many."

"Well, maybe he was really hungry," Margaret said, trying to be funny.

"Well, he did and they're all gone, huh, Mommy?" said Paulie.

"No, honey, we still have a lot left, so everyone just sit down and behave yourselves."

"Yeah, all but Gary, cuz he already ate enough," Paulie said.

With all the commotion at that moment, Little Gary didn't know what to say. He was hurt and embarrassed by everyone's reaction and emotionally upset, so he walked out the back door unnoticed and sat on the porch, trying not to cry. He didn't want his sisters to see him crying, or even look as though he was about to cry, or they would have teased him like they had so many times in the past. Besides, if his friends found out they, too, would have surely teased him.

Instead, Little Gary held back his tears and began thinking about how great it was going to be the next two weeks hanging out with his best friends and all the fun they were going to have before going back to school.

Then, slightly grinning, Little Gary licked his lips and thought to himself, *Man, those beans were really good. I hope there's still some left for later.*

Final Days
chapter four

Sitting quietly alone on the back porch with his back propped up against the screen door, as he had often done when wanting to be alone with his thoughts, Little Gary thought about all the fun times he'd shared with his best friends, Roy, Johnny, and Leonard, and how sad it was going to be to leave them. His mother had just learned they'd been accepted into the housing projects on the other side of town, and she was waiting to hear when they could officially move.

The application for government housing she had submitted two years earlier had finally made it through the maze of bureaucracy. And finally, after years of living in cramped quarters and other crowded housing conditions, Little Gary and his family were moving to a more suitable and healthier living environment.

I'm never going to see my friends again, Little Gary thought as he reminisced about his life on Wyandot Street. He had been friends with Roy, Leonard, and Johnny since before starting first grade, and the thought of moving away was somewhat overwhelming.

All four boys were now in the fourth grade and were inseparable. They did everything together it seemed, from selling newspapers on the street corner in the downtown area and at the ballpark on weekends to swimming naked in the North Platte River that ran parallel along the highway near where they lived. They spent countless hours playing Cowboys and Indians in Roy's backyard and war games chucking dirt clods at one another, as if they were hand grenades, in the weedy vacant lots till all hours of the night.

Soon this will all end, he thought: no more playing hide-and-seek, Kick the Can, telling spooky stories late at night in Roy's basement, or talking about girls, especially Gloria, who they all had a crush on but forever denied it.

Then there was Officer Young, the motorcycle policeman, whom they gathered around in evenings to hear of his stories of wild car chases and experiences as a police officer.

"Why do we have to move?" Little Gary asked, with his head tilted back, looking up as if waiting for an answer. "I don't want to move," he continued talking to himself. "I like living here. Maybe I could live with Roy cuz he doesn't live with his mom and dad. I wish I had a Grandma and Grandpa to live with, then I could stay here with my friends."

No one knew why Roy lived with his grandparents. All that anyone ever knew was that his parents lived on the other side of town in a nice house in a nice neighborhood; that he had two younger sisters, a younger brother, and a father who worked building houses. All the neighborhood kids thought Roy's family was rich and wondered why he didn't live with them, but no one had ever asked. Sometimes, during the summer months, he would invite us to spend the weekend at his parents' house, where we would sleep outside in the front yard, staring up at the stars and talking about our favorite topic, girls.

Moving to another part of town was not only a sad moment for Little Gary but for his mother as well. She had grown very comfortable with the neighborhood and had formed close relationships with her neighbors, especially Leonard's and Johnny's family, who all lived in the same two-story house.

On occasion, when times were extremely hard, the families shared resources and offered support to one another. There was one time, she remembered, when she had gone grocery shopping and made arrangements to have the groceries delivered to her house so that she could go directly to work from the grocery store. Upon returning home later that evening, she found Little Gary waiting up for her, like he had done on many occasions. "Were the groceries delivered?" she remembered asking him.

"What groceries?" was Little Gary's answer.

"The groceries I had delivered today. Were they delivered?"

"We didn't get any groceries, but they got groceries next door cuz they were all eating oranges and stuff while we watched."

The groceries, it turned out, were delivered to Leonard's house by mistake earlier that afternoon, when Leonard's mother was out, and it wasn't discovered until later that evening. The next morning his mother felt bad about what had happened, and over coffee with Leonard's mother, enjoyed a laugh about the incident as their sons played in the yard.

While there were other memorable moments about the neighborhood that came to mind as his mother was preparing for the move, the overwhelming factor that precipitated moving was the family's poor living conditions, which bear mentioning again. It was unsuitable and unbearable for a family of nine to be living in three rooms in an overcrowded three-family housing unit heated only by woodburning stoves.

Though there was electricity throughout the housing unit, it was used only for lighting, which meant when it came to doing laundry and bathing, water had to be heated on a wood-and-coal-burning stove, where cooking was also done. And to keep food from spoiling, blocks of ice had to be purchased and placed in an icebox for refrigeration. Of all the hardships the family had to bear while living in such dire conditions, the worst was having to go outside to use the toilet in the coal shed, shared by twenty-four people. More alarming was the cesspool (a large septic tank) and the danger it posed, located in the garage just outside the back door where Little Gary's family lived.

It was his mother's dream of finding suitable housing for her husband and seven children, where the living conditions were safe and healthy, and equipped with all the necessities and amenities of modern-day living, such as indoor plumbing, heating, bathroom facilities, and appliances for cooking and refrigeration, all of which were missing where they had been living over the past several years.

Little Gary's mother's prayers had now been answered: no more cold winter nights watching her children huddled together, shivering underneath skimpy blankets, trying to keep warm; and no more going outside late at night to the toilet in a drafty shed while keeping an eye out for anyone who might be lurking around; and no more depending on Little Gary to chop wood or haul ice from the ice-vending machine several blocks away.

Yes, life would be different for Little Gary and his family. Although they would not be moving into a single dwelling, the new location was a godsend. Each unit in the projects had two or three bedrooms, a kitchen, a living room, and a bathroom, and was fully equipped with central heating and appliances. To Little Gary's mother's surprise, however, the unit they were assigned was the exception in that it came with five bedrooms. Only one other unit throughout the entire housing complex had five bedrooms as well and was also assigned to a family of nine. Not only would the family, for the first time, have plenty of living space and be surrounded by comfortable living conditions, but there was a Catholic school across the alley from the family's back door and a Catholic church one block away. *Another prayer answered,* his mother thought when she heard the surprising news. She had always wanted to send her children to Catholic school, and now she had the opportunity to do so. Her only concern now was would she be able to afford the tuition. Like everything else, she would leave it in God's hands.

"Garr, what are you doing sitting alone on the porch in this dark, dingy garage? We've been waiting for you at Roy's. Don't you wanna go with us to the Platte for a swim, so we can try out the diving board we made?" Leonard asked.

"Nah, I don't think so. I don't feel like it right now."

"Why not, man? You were all excited earlier when we talked about it," Roy asked.

"Well, I changed my mind and I don't wanna go, so don't bug me."

"Damn, man, what's bugging you? Let's split, guys. Gary's being a butthead," Roy said.

"Come on, Garr, go with us," Johnny intervened.

"Yeah, Garr, go with us," Leonard repeated. "What's wrong, man?" he asked sympathetically.

"I, I just found out we're moving," Little Gary said quietly.

"Moving? What do you mean you're moving? Moving where?" Leonard asked, surprised.

"To the East side," Little Gary answered.

"To the East side?" Leonard responded. "You mean, you guys are moving from the West side to the East side? Damn, man, you're gonna be an Eastsider and we're gonna be Westsiders. Wow! You know what that means."

"No! What does that mean?" Little Gary asked somewhat angrily.

"It means we're gonna be enemies."

"What are you even talking about, enemies?" Little

Gary asked with a disturbed tone in his voice. "You don't know what you're talking about."

"Yeah I do. That's when the Eastside gangs fight with the Westside gangs."

It turns out Leonard had overheard his older brother, Victor, talking to his buddies about a gang fight with the Eastsiders that was going to take place at one of the parks. Leonard didn't really understand the whole territorial rival concept of gang fighting between different parts of the inner city and was only trying to convey what he had overheard.

"Come on, you guys, let's go," Roy interrupted. "Besides, this might be the last time Gary will be able to go with us. Right, Garr?"

"Well, maybe a few more times; we aren't moving today," said Little Gary, now in a more positive mood.

Nothing more was mentioned that day about moving. Little Gary didn't talk about it and the guys didn't bring it up. That day, along with a few more that summer, was spent swimming in the North Platte River and bouncing off their makeshift diving board underneath the Eighth Avenue Bridge as cars and trucks crossed over.

The next several days, Little Gary moped around the house feeling sad, knowing that in just a few weeks he would be leaving his friends and the neighborhood, perhaps forever. When his mother asked what was wrong, and why he wasn't outside playing with his friends, all he would say was, "I don't feel like it." But his mother knew; she was just waiting for him to open up and talk about it.

In fact, her three daughters also seemed a bit upset

about their impending move but also didn't talk to her about it. The other three children, Paulie and the twins, Danny and Donny, were too young to understand what was happening.

As for Little Gary's father, he was looking forward to the move. He thought that by moving to another environment his situation would change for the better; that he would cut down on this drinking and find permanent employment that was more suitable and commensurate with his skills as an ironworker. He was tired of the menial work he subjected himself to due to his drinking. He genuinely wanted to change his pattern of failing to that of being a responsible father and husband. Though he loved his family very much, he was unable to express it openly. The reality of his situation was chronic alcoholism, and he needed professional treatment to overcome his addiction but was reluctant to seek help.

Several weeks passed and his mother still hadn't been notified as to when the move would take place. *Maybe something is wrong,* she thought. *Maybe they gave our housing unit to another, more deserving, family. Or maybe we didn't meet the eligibility criteria after all.* Reflecting back to the interview process with the housing authority, she remembered one major issue that nearly disqualified the family from being considered for low-income housing, and that was her husband's occupation. The salary structure for ironworkers was above the average wage rate compared to other workers with different job skills.

However, at the time his mother submitted the application for low-income housing, her husband, due to his alcoholism, had been unemployed for the past six months with no end in sight of ever returning to his craft and, as a result, was forced to accept menial low-paying jobs, which, to him, were demeaning. In a way, he used this predicament as an excuse to further perpetuate his alcohol addiction. Thereby, the family was able to meet the socially disadvantaged criteria for government housing. *But this had already been explained and documented,* she thought to herself. *So why haven't we heard from the housing authority? It must be something else, but what?*

Had it not been for his drinking, because of his skill as an ironworker, Little Gary's father could have provided a comfortable living in a middle-class setting for his family. But then again, there could have been a whole set of different circumstances one would rather not experience. Little Gary's father, when he wasn't drinking, was good-looking, well liked, charming, and fun to be around. His drinking, unfortunately, had such a strong hold on him that he missed out on many employment opportunities, lost the respect of friends and relatives, and alienated his family to the point of their being ashamed, embarrassed, and often times, fearful of his behavior, though he was not physically abusive. The one person, however, who never gave up on him was his wife. She loved her husband very much and tried in every way to help him overcome his alcohol addiction. She offered an admirable example for how to treat one of God's children gone astray.

Two more weeks had passed and still no word from the housing authority, so Mrs. Trujillo paid a visit to the district office to inquire as to why she hadn't been notified when to move. To her surprise, she was informed they had sent her a letter four weeks earlier stating she had thirty days to accept the offer of a five-bedroom housing unit or it would be offered to another applicant.

"But I never received the letter," Mrs. Trujillo responded frantically to the district housing clerk.

"Well, we sent it," the clerk replied sternly. "And you have two days to officially notify this office of your acceptance; after that you will have to reapply," she continued in a condescending and rude manner.

"Well, since I'm here now, may I sign the office's copy of the acceptance letter?" Mrs. Trujillo politely asked.

Still somewhat perturbed, the clerk blurted out, "No, there are no provisions in a situation like this."

"Well, there must be something that can be done. Isn't there? Could you at least find out from your supervisor or whoever is in charge if I could sign the acceptance letter today since I'm standing right here in your office? Otherwise, there is no way I could ever meet the deadline and we've waited over two years for this opportunity to find decent housing. Please, is there anything you can do?"

"Wait here, then," the clerk rudely instructed Mrs. Trujillo. "I'll have to go ask my supervisor. I'll be right back."

"Thank you very much, I really appreciate you doing this," said Mrs. Trujillo.

As the clerk approached her supervisor's office, she knocked on the door twice and entered. Then, as the door was closing behind her, Mrs. Trujillo could hear a man's voice utter in an angry manner, "Beth, why on earth are you so . . ." and the door shut.

Thinking to herself, Mrs. Trujillo still could not understand what could have happened to the housing notification letter. She had checked the mail daily for the letter over the past several weeks and was sure it hadn't arrived. Then a puzzled look came over her as she quietly said to herself, "I wonder if . . . no, he wouldn't do such a thing." For an instant, she thought that perhaps Little Gary had taken the letter from the mailbox. It bothered her to even think her son would entertain such a thought, let alone act on it. He had been somewhat secretive and quiet the past few weeks, she remembered.

"Ma'am, ma'am," the clerk said in a high-pitched voice, but this time the tone in her voice was more civil.

"Oh, I'm sorry, Miss. I was just thinking about what could have happened to the letter that was sent."

"I talked to my supervisor and he's going to allow you to sign our copy of the letter. You need to know, however, that this is not normally permitted. But given the circumstances, he has authorized it. I'm sure it would have been devastating to you had you missed the deadline."

"Yes, you have no idea how devastating. I really appreciate your assistance and apologize for any inconvenience. Thank you so much."

As Mrs. Trujillo read the letter, she was taken aback. "It says here we have until the end of the month to move or be placed back on the waiting list for the next available housing unit. This only gives us two weeks to move," she said to the clerk. "Is it possible to get an extension of two weeks beyond the two weeks we have?"

"I'm afraid not, Mrs. Trujillo. Once deadlines are set, they must be adhered to due to strict housing scheduling issues. I'm sorry."

Mrs. Trujillo didn't want to push further and ask to speak to the clerk's supervisor for a final decision, but instead said, "Well, I guess I better start making arrangements to move. It would be a shame to lose out on this opportunity after having waited so long. Thank you again, Miss . . , by the way, what is your name?" she asked the clerk as she handed back her signed housing acceptance letter.

"Beth Morgan," the clerk answered. "And I hope all goes well with you, Mrs. Trujillo," she said sympathetically.

"Thank you, Miss Morgan."

Later that evening, during supper, his mother informed the children of her visit with the housing authority. As she explained the situation, she noticed Little Gary with his head bent down and fidgeting nervously, so she decided not to elaborate too much on what precipitated her visit, thinking perhaps he knew something about the missing letter. So she merely explained that they had two weeks to move—a lot had to be done—and everyone was expected to pitch in and help.

"But I don't want to move," Little Gary's eldest sister said. "Does this mean we have to go to another school?"

"Yes, Cindy, but in your case you can finish out the school year here. But then you will have to attend one of the high schools near where we will be living. As for the rest of you kids, you will have to transfer to another school." She didn't want to say she had intentions of sending them to a Catholic school.

"But why do we have to change schools?" Frances and Margaret both asked.

"Because the both of you are still in middle school and I'm not going to have all three of you travel across town to go to school, so the both of you will have to transfer."

But rather than react to her daughters' disappointment, she simply conveyed to the children how much nicer it was going to be to finally have indoor plumbing and electricity throughout the whole house to heat all the rooms and warm the water for baths. "And imagine," she continued, "no more going outside late at night in the dead of winter just to go to the bathroom. That alone will be worth it, don't you think?" But it wasn't until she mentioned the number of bedrooms they were going to have that their faces lit up and they began to listen more intently.

"Oh, wow!" yelled Margaret, "I get my own bedroom?"

"Not so fast, Margaret," her mother said. "You and Frances will need to share a bedroom. The twins will have their own bedroom. And Gary and Paul will share a bedroom. As for Cindy, since she is the oldest, she will be the only one to have her own bedroom. And your dad and I will have our own bedroom. Just think, we're going from one bedroom to five bedrooms. We might even get lost with all those bedrooms," his mother said jokingly.

Over the next two weeks, his mother was extremely busy organizing the move during the day and working long hours at the hospital at night; though she elicited the help of her neighbor, Mrs. Benavidez, to help with all the moving arrangements since her daughters were at school and could only be helpful in the evenings.

Meanwhile, word was out throughout the neighborhood that the Trujillo family was moving to the housing projects on the other side of town.

"What are the housing projects?" Leonard asked. "And why didn't you tell us you were moving?"

"What do you mean, *pendejo*, why I didn't tell you? I told you guys a long time ago I was moving to the East side, but you didn't believe me."

"No, you didn't," Leonard said.

"Yes, I did."

"No, you didn't."

"Yes, I did, so get over it."

"Hey, what's going on; you guys fighting?" asked Johnny. But before they had a chance to respond, Johnny hollered out, "Hey, Roy, Garr and Leonard are gonna throw *chingasos*."

"*Odaley*, I gotta see this," Roy said, as he ran across the street to where Little Gary and Leonard were standing.

Seconds later, several more neighborhood kids came running down the street, yelling from the top of their lungs, "A fight! A fight!"

"Hey, wait a minute, we aren't fighting," said Little Gary. "Leonard's just being a butt."

"Yeah well, you're the butt, you butthead," Leonard snapped back.

"Deck him one," someone yelled out from the group of kids that had gathered to see a fight.

"I said we ain't fighting," Little Gary repeated as he angrily walked past the mob of onlookers and disappeared behind his house. Followed by Leonard, who went home.

"Okay, everybody, split; no fighting today unless one of you *cabróns* want to throw *chingasos* with me," Roy said, bravely beating his chest.

"Say, what's up with Garr?" Johnny asked Roy.

"Don't you remember he told us he was moving and we didn't believe him? That's what he and Leonard were arguing about. I guess Leonard forgot he had told us. That's what's bothering him. He's pretty upset about it."

"Damn, I don't want him to move," Johnny said.

"I don't either," said Roy. "Let's go talk to him; maybe we can cheer him up or something. Let's get Leonard."

Walking toward the back of the garage where Little Gary lived, the boys found him standing up against the neighbors' fence, looking down at the ground.

"Garr, we know you're sad about moving, but it won't be for a few weeks, right?" Roy asked.

"No, we have to move in two weeks, and I really don't want to talk about it."

"Hey, man, I'm sorry we almost got in a fight," Leonard said, walking up to him as he placed his arm around Little Gary's shoulder.

"Yeah, man, we really don't want you to move," Johnny and Roy said as they, too, walked up to Little Gary and affectionately patted him on the back.

"Heck, we're still gonna be friends; right, guys?" said Roy.

"Hell yeah," Johnny said. "We just have to know where you're gonna be living, so we could go visit you."

"Yeah, then we could hang out over at your pad and meet some, you know," Leonard said, raising his eyebrows up and down in a rapid motion.

"What are you talking about, Leonard?" said Johnny. "Every time you even get close to a girl, you get all *skamau* and start stuttering."

"I do not."

"You sure as hell do," Roy said, jumping in. "What about the time you bumped into Gloria in the hallway at school? You got all shaky and couldn't even talk."

"Yeah, but what about that time we saw Gloria at the park?" Leonard said. "You and Johnny fell all over yourselves and couldn't even walk straight."

"I remember that time," Little Gary joined in, in defense of Leonard, and with a large grin on his face, said, "You guys did fall all over yourselves, and if Gloria was any closer you two *pendejos* would have fainted."

"Yeah, so who's the one that's *skamau*?" said Leonard.

For the next few minutes the four friends continued to tease each other, as they had on so many other occasions, and laughter filled the air as they huddled together in solidarity.

It was at that moment Little Gary knew that although distance would separate him from his friends, his memory of them would never fade.

Two weeks later, Little Gary was gone.

The author, Gary (*left*), and his childrood friend, Roy (*right*), in 1953.

The Move

chapter five

Soon turning eleven years old, Little Gary had never traveled any great distance from his neighborhood nor had he ever experienced the joy of riding in the back of a truck. The closest Little Gary ever came to this kind of excitement was when he and his friends were driven home in the newspaper van from the baseball stadium where they sold the *Saturday Evening Post* on game night.

Holding on tightly to a bedpost, teary-eyed Little Gary waved goodbye to Roy, Johnny, and Leonard, who were standing at the end of the block, waving their goodbyes in silence, since they were too choked up to say anything. Moments later, the truck Little Gary was riding in, reached the top of the viaduct and disappeared.

Never had it occurred to Little Gary and his friends that they would ever be separated. The only time any one of them was ever apart was on occasions when Roy would spend the weekend at his parents' home, or when Little Gary would visit his cousins, Joyce and Judy, who lived on the East side of town close to where he and his family were moving.

Little Gary loved visiting his cousins, both of whom were near his age. They lived in a single-family two-bedroom house with all the amenities of comfortable living. Unlike where Little Gary had lived, his cousins had their own indoor bathroom, hot running water, electrical appliances, and a system circulating heat throughout the house on those cold winter nights.

The one thing Little Gary really looked forward to during his visits was the choice he had in selecting the type of cereal he was going to eat for breakfast, whereas at home, breakfast usually consisted of Corn Flakes mixed in with oatmeal, or on occasion scrambled eggs and tortillas.

What he dreaded the most, though, about visiting his cousins was the long drive back home on Sunday evening, sitting in the back seat of his uncle's car, wishing these visits would never come to an end.

As for Little Gary's friends who were left behind: "What do you guys wanna do now?" asked Leonard. "Let's go swimming at the Platte."

"Nah," Roy said. "I'm gonna split home."

"Yeah, me too," said Johnny. "I don't feel like doing anything."

"Come on, you guys, let's do something," insisted Leonard.

Not responding, Roy and Johnny slowly drifted off in different directions, leaving Leonard feeling sad and alone as he glanced toward the viaduct for one last look, with tears about to roll down his face, wondering if he would ever see Little Gary again.

Sitting up against the cab of the truck in between

boxes of clothes and furniture, the realization of moving had not yet fazed Little Gary. So many thoughts were going through his mind he didn't know what to think. The only thing he was sure of was that he was leaving his best friends, and at that moment it was painful.

"Are you okay back there, Gary?" he could hear his father asking from inside the truck.

"Yeah, I'm okay," Little Gary said in a low voice.

"What? I can't hear you," his father shouted back.

"I'm okay," he responded again, only this time much louder.

Little Gary had always spoken very softly and under his breath, to the point that he could hardly be heard. His father would say to him, "Speak up, boy, I can't hear you." And his sisters would tease him to no end when they couldn't hear what he was saying. They would often call out to their mother, "Gary's lips are moving, but there's no sound coming out of his mouth. He must be deaf and dumb because we cannot hear a word he's saying." Then they would run outside laughing before their mother could respond.

Oftentimes Little Gary's sisters' behavior toward him would hurt his feelings and he would cry, which made the situation even worse, because his sisters would then call him a "crybaby." Even in later years he was confronted with this situation. Like the time when he was in the eighth grade and his teacher, Sister Ruth Marian, asked him to go to the blackboard to work out a math problem, his favorite subject, and when he arrived at the answer she asked him how he came up with it.

He then explained the mathematical steps he took to

solve the problem, but did so in a very quiet manner. At which point the Sister said she couldn't hear him and doubted whether the other students could either, so she again, only this time in a more frustrating way, asked him how he came up with the answer. She told him the answer was correct, but that she and the rest of the class still couldn't hear his explanation; he needed to speak up.

So again, Gary proceeded to explain how he arrived at the correct answer, but only to be interrupted by the Sister telling him, in a scolding way, "Gary, go back to your desk, collect your books and supplies, and head over to Sister Ann Jude's class. I'll explain to you and the Sister after class why I'm sending you back to the seventh grade." Or like the many times, as his wife tells it, when they were dating in high school and he would call her on the telephone. She knew exactly who was calling when one of her siblings would answer the phone and shout out, "What? Who is this? I can't hear you."

The drive to their new home seemed like a long and great distance to Little Gary, since this was his first trip sitting in back of the truck with the last load of furniture to be moved. His father and Leonard's uncle, Juan Gomez, had already made several trips earlier that day, given that Mr. Gomez's truck was a small pickup with limited load capacity.

Little Gary could see the tall buildings as they drove through the center of town, stopping every one or two blocks for traffic lights. As he gazed at all the sights, he found himself wondering what his new surroundings would be like. Would he make friends quickly? Would he like his new school? And what are the "projects" that he heard his mother talk so much about to Leonard's mother, which they were moving into?

Suddenly the truck came to an abrupt stop, followed by a moment of silence, then the sound of voices echoed in the air. "Well, this is it, *compadre*, no more trips back to that dump of a place you guys lived in for six years."

"Yeah, *compadre*," said Little Gary's father, "this is quite a change from the slums. You guys were smart to move out when you did."

"Yeah, Josie and I still remember what it was like. We were fortunate to find a house near the job and in the same school district so the kids didn't have to change schools. You guys are really going to enjoy it here. And the grass, it's everywhere, *hombre*. How you going to cut it? You don't even have a lawn mower, *hombre*."

"*No problema, viejo*, lawn mowers are kept at the maintenance office for tenant use only. And it ain't me who's going to do the cutting; it's him," Little Gary's father said, pointing to the back of the truck as he and his friend stepped out.

"Okay, Gary, we're here. Here's the key to the house. Go open the door, and hold the screen door open while we unload the furniture," said Little Gary's father.

Slowly lifting himself up from the bed of the truck, Little Gary peeked over the side of the truck railing, as if trying not to be seen, and looked all around in amazement. He couldn't believe his eyes—multiple two-story redbrick buildings that lined the street for what seemed like miles. "Wow, I guess these are the projects," he said in a low voice, not wanting to be heard. "They sure are big. And there's grass everywhere and no dirt streets."

This was something spectacular to Little Gary, since the neighborhood where he'd lived for several years was surrounded by unpaved dusty roads and weedy vacant lots.

Suddenly his thoughts turned to Roy, Johnny, and Leonard. *Gee, I wish the guys could see this. We could really have fun wrestling on the grass and not get all dirty like we did when we wrestled on the dirt roads.* Not knowing, of course, anything about grass stains.

"Well, *viejo*, let's start unloading," Mr. Gomez said, "or the longer I stay, I'll be moving in with you."

"Muy bien, compadre," answered Little Gary's father.

Little Gary still couldn't believe what he was seeing, but he jumped down from the back of the truck and walked slowly, as if in a daze, toward the front door and onto the cement porch of their new house.

"Gary, stop daydreaming and get the door open," his father yelled out. "That kid," he mumbled to Mr. Gomez.

"Well, *viejo*, you have to understand this is all so strange to him. Everything about this place is different. Eight rooms, inside bathroom, appliances. Man, this is quite a shock compared to what you left behind. Wouldn't you say?"

"Yeah, *hombre*, it is different all right. The one nice thing, though, no more having to go outside to *el baño*, especially in the dead of winter."

"Ain't that the truth," said Mr. Gomez. "I remember those days. Come on, *viejo*, let's finish up here so we can down a few."

"I'm for that," Little Gary's father responded.

Shortly after, his mother, brothers, and sisters pulled

up in a station wagon, all crunched up, driven by their neighbor, Mrs. Ortega, who, with her husband, owned and operated a fruit and vegetable market in their old neighborhood. The Ortegas were considered the wealthy neighbors because they were business owners. In fact, very few of the neighborhood residents even owned a vehicle, let alone a business.

"Mother, this place is awful," Cindy said. "I don't want to live here. Just look at all these ugly redbrick buildings. It looks like a prison here."

"Well then, I tell you what," her mother said, "after you help get everything into the house, you can go back to where we came from, okay?"

"Come on, Cindy," Mrs. Ortega joined in, with intentions of humoring her, "let's unload the car, then I'll take you back to your old neighborhood and maybe one of your neighbors will let you stay with them until you finish high school."

"Well then, if Cindy's going back, I want to go too," said Frances.

"Me too," Margaret joined in. "I don't like it here either."

"Fine then, if all three of you want to go back to where we came from, then as soon as you are finished here you can get your belongings and maybe Mrs. Ortega will take you back and maybe, just maybe, one of your friends' mothers will let you move in with them. Although you may not be able to stay together if you don't find someone to take you all in."

"Mommy," Paulie tugged on his mother's dress, "I don't want to go back. It's pretty here."

"We don't either," the six-year-old twins both said. "It's really pretty here."

"You guys don't know what you like; you're too young," Cindy told them.

"Yeah, well, you're too old to know anything," one of the boys shot back.

"Okay, okay, kids, that's enough out of you. Let's get everything moved into the house," their mother said with irritation.

"Hey, you guys," Little Gary yelled out to his siblings from the second-story window, leaning halfway out. "Wait till you see this place; it's huge. It's like a mansion, and we each have our own bedroom."

"A lot of good that does," uttered Cindy under her breath. "We don't even have any real beds to fill all those rooms, only those old iron rollaway beds and a couch we've been sleeping on."

Overhearing her, Danny, one of the twins, said very innocently, "I thought you didn't want to live with us?"

"Oh be quiet!" Cindy snapped back.

"Mother," Margaret shouted, "Gary is climbing out the window, and he's gonna fall and break his skinny little neck."

"Oh, Margaret, stop exaggerating and finish helping your sisters with the rest of the bags."

"Yeah, Margaret, stop exaggerating," Frances repeated, "and stop trying to get out of helping us. You always seem to disappear when it comes time to do things. Like when we were getting ready to move, you were nowhere to be found so Cindy and I ended up doing all the packing and cleanup before leaving."

"And you like to disobey at times," Cindy chimed in. "When Mom tells you to do something, you say you will but then you won't."

Margaret did have a tendency to get out of doing things and allow her imagination to get the best of her. A few years back, as you recall, she and Little Gary were practically run over by a truck while crossing the street after visiting the store to buy some candy. Even though she ended up in the hospital due to a head injury, she made it sound, to her friends, as if it were a life-and-death situation, telling them that she was trapped under the truck for hours and unconscious until the firemen freed her. She had disobeyed her mother that day and talked Little Gary into going with her to the store.

Once everything had been moved in, their mother gave Mrs. Ortega a tour of the house while their father and Mr. Gomez sat out on the back porch, drinking beer and discussing the new environment.

"Very, very nice," Mrs. Ortega said to their mother. "It's hard to believe that the nine of you lived in that three-room house for all those years without indoor heating and plumbing, and worst of all having to go outside just to go to the bathroom. That must have really been something."

"Yes, this is quite a change. Like Gary said, this place is a 'mansion' compared to where we lived. And what is so wonderful, the church is only a block away and the school is right across the alley. A Catholic school, mind you, where I've always wanted to send the kids. Yes, we are very fortunate and blessed."

"I am so happy for you to have found suitable housing.

I wish you all the best," said Mrs. Ortega.

"Gracias, mi amiga," their mother said with heartfelt appreciation.

"Cindy, Frances, Margaret, we're leaving now," Mrs. Ortega called out while smiling as she walked toward the front door. "Get your belongings and say goodbye to your mother and brothers."

"Shhh" was the sound coming from the upstairs.

"Hmm, I guess they changed their minds," Mrs. Trujillo said, also smiling. "Maybe they're going to like it here after all."

"She's leaving now," Cindy whispered to her sisters as they all slowly raised their heads above the window ledge to see Mrs. Ortega leave.

"Well, *compadre, una más cerveza y ya me voy*," said Mr. Gomez.

But for Little Gary's father one more beer led to another, and another, and then he would switch to wine, which he strongly favored to the point of dependency, and by evening's end he would end up sprawled out on the sofa, passed out. This always brought a sense of sadness to his mother to see her husband in that condition.

Although Little Gary's father was a skilled ironworker and earned an above-average wage when he was employed, he could not hold down a job for any given length of time because of his drinking. His promises to his wife to quit were many, but his attempts to fulfill them were overcome by an addiction so strong that his day-to-day existence was dependent on that next drink.

Quite often Little Gary's father would call on him to serve him a glass of wine. He would say quietly, "Gary, *dame un traguito,*" while measuring with his thumb and index finger the amount. Sometimes, though, without saying a word, if Little Gary was in sight, his father would merely hold up his hand, gesturing with his thumb and index finger, and Little Gary would immediately reach behind the sofa and pull up a half-full bottle of Midwest Tokay wine his father had hidden away so as not to be seen by the smaller children. Though it was no secret to anyone in the household what was hidden behind the sofa.

That evening, after everything had been put in its place and the bedrooms assigned, his mother sat at the kitchen table with a cup of coffee in her hand, silently thanking God for all that He had provided. *It's so comforting,* she thought, looking out the window at the Catholic school and the church, *to know that the children are safe in their rooms.* She couldn't get over how spacious their new dwelling was.

It's a new start, she continued thinking as she poured herself a second cup of coffee. *Now if only he would get help,* referring to her husband's drinking, *and find steady employment, this could be the beginning of a new and exciting life for us.* Then slowly bowing her head, she said, "But I will leave everything in your hands, O Lord."

"Mother, Cindy won't let us go into her room," Margaret called from the top of the stairs. "She said she was never going to let us step foot in her bedroom."

"Quiet, or you'll wake your father. You and Frances have your own bedroom, so there is no need to bother your sister. Now stop your whining and go back to your room."

How ironic, she thought, *only last night the children were sleeping in the living room on rollaway beds, and tonight they have four bedrooms to share among themselves. Life is good.*

A few minutes later Little Gary also called out from the top of the stairs, "Mom, when are we going to get beds?"

"Soon," his mother said. "Now go back to your room and go to sleep."

"We don't have a bed, remember?" Little Gary answered back. "We have a rollaway. Can we also get a television?"

"We have more important things to get first, now go to sleep. We'll talk about it in the morning."

"Did you hear, you guys? We're gonna get a TV," Little Gary said as he poked his head into the girls' room.

"Oh, wow! Then I won't have to go ask the neighbors if we can watch their TV," Margaret said, "like I used to."

"What do you mean, you," Little Gary burst out. "I'm the one that would always go ask if we could watch their television. All you ever did was hide somewhere and make me do it."

"Yeah, but I'm the one who had the idea."

"Oh, you're full of it," Little Gary said and went back to the bedroom he shared with his younger brother Paul.

"Are we really gonna get a TV?" his brother asked.

"Sure are," Little Gary said with confidence.

"Do you think if we do, they will take it back like they did the first time we got a TV, remember?" Paul asked him.

"Nah, not this time," he assured his little brother.

"Wow! Then we could watch *The Lone Ranger* and

cartoons and Captain Ozie Waters."

"Yeah, I can hardly wait," responded Little Gary.

"Yeah, me too," said Paul. "Remember when Leonard had a TV and we would look through the hole in the wall and they didn't even know we were doing that? But then something happened to the peephole and we couldn't look through it anymore."

"They knew," Little Gary said. "That's why they plugged it up."

Paul was eight years old and pretty much stayed close to the house, never venturing off like Little Gary did when he was with his friends. He seemed to always stay close to his mother and follow her around the house when she wasn't working. Wherever she went he was practically hanging on to her. If she were to suddenly stop and turn around, Paul would run into her.

For the rest of the evening, everything was quiet. Frances and Margaret were in their room, talking softly. Cindy was in her room, quietly humming a favorite tune. The six-year-old twins, Danny and Donny, were fast asleep. And Little Gary and Paulie were in their room, still talking about the television programs they were going to watch once they got a TV, which of course was not to be until sometime in the future.

Toward midnight, after his mother finally got her husband to go upstairs to bed, she made her rounds around their new house, making sure the doors were locked, the shades were drawn, and the kids were all in bed. It still seemed unreal to her that her family, for the first time, was living in suitable housing compared to their previous living conditions.

"Gary, why are you still up?" his mother asked as she poked in on him and Paul.

"I can't sleep," he said. "I keep thinking about Roy, Johnny, and Leonard. I wish they could have moved with us and lived next door so we could still hang out."

"Well, honey, you'll find new friends. It won't take long. Now go to sleep."

As she quietly closed the bedroom door, she could hear a soft whisper coming from Paulie: "Gary, are we still gonna get a TV?"

"Shhh, go to sleep."

Establishing Roots
chapter six

The next nine years were spent living in the projects, which were only a few miles from the slums where Little Gary grew up but miles apart from their poor living conditions. It was during this time that he matured into a sensible, responsible young adult as a result of his educational and religious teachings, which were developed while attending Catholic school.

Moving into government housing provided his family, for the first time, decent livable conditions. The move offered what his mother said it would: "plenty of bedrooms, an inside bathroom, modern cooking appliances, electric heating throughout all the rooms, and plenty of yard space." Never again did Gary ever have to chop wood or haul large blocks of ice to an antiquated icebox, as he did when he was a little boy. And no more taking turns to bathe in a makeshift tin bathtub since their new bathtub was the size of what Gary's younger brother, Danny, once called a "swimming pool." But best of all, was not having to make those late-night potty runs to the coal shed. All in all, living in the projects was a godsend.

Gary's mother was especially appreciative and extremely happy since now she had the opportunity to send the children to Catholic school. Even though the tuition at that time was only fifteen dollars for the school year, it was still considered a financial burden. But this would not stop her from seeing to it that her kids received a Catholic education. The two older daughters, Cindy and Frances, however, would continue their education in a public school.

As it turned out, though, Cindy quit school to work full-time, but later resumed her education and graduated from a Catholic school. Frances, on the other hand, dropped out of school altogether and spent all her time helping out at home. She cared for her younger siblings while their mother continued working the late shift at the hospital, which was not as far as it had been before moving. This meant their mother no longer had to face that long walk over the viaduct late at night.

It didn't take long for Gary to adapt to his new environment, though at times he longed to be back with Roy, Johnny, and Leonard. This longing for his old friends, however, gradually faded as he matured and developed new friendships. In fact, over time, he befriended not only his Catholic schoolmates but also some of the neighborhood kids that attended the nearby public school, with whom he hung out on weekends.

Gary had been dead set against going to Catholic school. But the two new groups of friends he surrounded himself with were due in part to his mother, who'd insisted he receive a Catholic education. After all, God had answered her prayers by placing them conveniently next to a Catholic grade school and a block away from a Catholic church.

So attending Catholic school took Gary a little time to get used too. What he found strange was the way the teachers dressed. They wore long black robes from head to toe, with white collars and a string of beads wrapped around their waists that hung down to the ground. Each morning, long before school began, these teachers would walk in double file to the church for morning Mass, which was a block away from the school. Gary would refer to them as "penguins," when describing them to his public school friends. And he had to address each individually as "Sister"; anything else would be considered disrespectful.

In addition to being taught by women dressed in black robes, Gary explained to his public school friends that they were also taught religion by priests that wore black suits and sometimes robes as well. This was all very strange to his friends, since most of them either weren't Catholic or never attended church.

Another odd practice Gary would tell his public school friends about was the school bell routine in the Catholic school system. Each morning before school started, while all the students were playing in the schoolyard, one of them would be selected to ring the school bell, which was gold-plated and handheld, weighing at least a pound. The student chosen for this prestigious task would then stand in front of the school entrance, holding on tightly with both hands to this strange-looking object so as not to drop it on the ground and thereby cause a mild earthquake. Once signaled by one of the teachers, the student would then begin ringing the bell several times by lifting their arm above their head, followed by a downward motion—careful not to break their wrist with each movement—until all the students in the schoolyard would come to an abrupt stop, taking a frozen-like position. Then once the entire student body maintained this position in dead silence the nuns would walk slowly between and around each frozen body to ensure total compliance of the "statue rule."

Then the "cowbell," as it was referred to, would sound a second time and all the frozen-like figures would quietly walk in total silence to their respective grade line, forming a single file facing the school building entrance. Following a third ringing of the bell, the students, in ranking order by grade level, would then march into the school, followed by the nuns, who watched the students' every move, ready to correct any inappropriate behavior. Any pushing or shoving by the students would not be tolerated, and if they did get caught misbehaving, they would be humiliated in front of the other students. Then, once in their respective classrooms, the nuns would select a student to begin the school day with a morning prayer.

"Wow! What a drag" was the usual reaction of Gary's public school friends when they learned of his Catholic school experience. At first Gary, too, was of the same opinion as his friends regarding the militaristic way in which the school operated. It wasn't long, however, before Gary was appreciative that his mother had enrolled him in Catholic school. Not only because he got the days off when holidays and holy days rolled around but, more importantly, because of the attention he received from the nuns and the priests, who seemed to care about his educational and spiritual direction as he continued his academic and religious education through high school.

It was during his high school years when Gary began developing a more full appreciation and understanding of who he was and what his responsibilities were as a young adult. His initiative, discipline, hard work, ambition, and the lessons he learned over the next several years and beyond were invaluable and are what prepared him for life's ups and downs, which he attributed to the values impressed upon him by his parents and the church. Gary's father was the disciplinarian in the physical sense, though not in a brutal way, conveying an awakening of understanding that any infraction of the rules carried consequences. It wasn't until his father died, at a very early age (forty-four), that Gary realized the love his father had for him but could only express in ways that seemed harsh and cruel. Gary's mother provided an example of all that was good and moral; she impressed upon him that good behavior would warrant positive outcomes in life. The pastor, Father Casey, a Jesuit priest at the church, was the disciplinarian in the religious sense and had a strong influence on Gary's obligation of obedience. These role models in Gary's life molded his entire being.

Graduating high school was Gary's first major milestone on his journey toward independence. It was clearly understood from the start that only a certain segment of high school students were college-bound, while the majority of the student population was either geared toward other postsecondary educational institutions, military service, or simply ignored due to a perceived lack of ambition. These were the options. So on "Career Day," if a student had high grades and showed strong academic potential, then they were encouraged to visit with college recruiters, while the remaining student body was given the choice of visiting with representatives from various local trade schools or recruiters from all four branches of the military.

Gary, at the time, did not have any specific plans beyond high school, though he knew from the outset that college was not an option considering his low grade point average of 2.3, which was not exactly "earth-shattering." Besides, no one in his family had ever attended college nor did he know anyone who had. In fact, the attitude among family and friends toward going to college was that only "rich white" people went to college; poor people of Mexican descent either went to a trade school, the military, or worked in dead-end jobs. It seemed as though one's neighborhood, nationality, and economic status were the indicators as to whether higher education was a reality or a dream. As for Gary, after high school, he thought of only getting a job to see where that would take him. He did not have any definite future plans.

Gary, from a very early age, had established a strong work ethic. He sold newspapers on the street corner downtown and at the baseball stadium on weekends at the ages of nine and ten. He had a paper route, delivering newspapers in and around his neighborhood, when he was eleven years old. Then, when he was twelve and thirteen, he worked at a local grocery store, off and on, stacking pop bottles, cleaning the meat-sawing machine, sweeping, and on occasion, waiting on customers.

While in high school, when many of his friends were involved in sports, Gary continued working though he was a member of the boxing team for three of his high school years. At one point he even tried out for football but soon realized the position he was assigned, it seemed, was to keep the bench warm for the other players and hand out oranges during half-time. While the rest of the players had grass stains on their uniforms Gary and his friend, Ernie, had orange stains on theirs. Then the unexpected happened midway through the football season. It was late in the fourth quarter when Coach Moore yelled out, "Gary! Ernie! Get your butts over here." At the urgent sound of his voice they scrambled around falling all over themselves looking for their helmets. As they ran toward the Coach, nervously adjusting their helmets, Coach said "Get your butts in there and help Gunner off the field." Dwayne (a.k.a. Gunner) was an outstanding athlete in all sports and very popular with the students. After this embarrassing moment in front of God and the fans, Gary quit football and resumed working.

He worked after school, on weekends, and during summer break. By the time he graduated he had held multiple part-time jobs: watering grass for a landscaper, packaging Can-a-Pop and driving a forklift at a pop company, busing tables and dish washing at a hotel restaurant, cleaning bricks at various construction sites, and delivering messages for Western Union, that is until his bicycle was stolen. Also, to help his mother pay for his tuition, Gary worked at various times for the nuns at school, running errands of some sort or another.

Within twenty-seven days after graduating high school, with no commitments or pending employment, the military became an option. So Gary and a very close friend, Dwayne, on a whim decided to join the US Army. As it turned out, though, Gary ended up serving a three-year term in Uncle Sam's Army. The way in which it happened is comical, to say the least, and bears telling.

On a summer day, toward the end of June 1962, Gary and his friend, Dwayne, were playing table tennis on the dining room table in Dwayne's house. Then, out of the blue, Gary said to his friend, "Let's join the army, but let's volunteer for the draft since it's only two years and not three."

"Okay, let's do it," said Dwayne, "but first let's go get Roy, since he's not doing anything either. Then we can all be together."

Roy was a high school friend of theirs (not to be confused with Gary's childhood friend, Roy), with whom they graduated. So the two friends went over to Roy's house to invite him to join them. Without hesitation Roy gladly accepted their invitation and off they went to the Custom House to join the army by volunteering for the draft.

"What do you think the guys are going to say when you two aren't around to play basketball with them?" Gary asked.

"Hell, I don't give a sh--," Roy said. "They can go f--- themselves." Roy was one of those kids whose every other word was a curse word. He didn't seem to care where he was or who was around him, except of course a certain priest, who would grab them by the collar and rattle every bone in their body if he heard any profanity from any of the guys.

"So, what about you, Dwayne, are you gonna miss it?" Gary asked.

"Nah, I don't think so," he replied. "It'll be cool, the three of us joining together. We're gonna have a great time. Maybe we'll be sent to all kinds of exotic places like Artie's brother. Remember him telling the guys all about the traveling he did when he was home on leave? So where do you think we'll be sent for basic training?"

"Hell, I don't give a sh--, I just wanna get the f--- out of this town," Roy blurted out.

"It's probably going to be Fort Carson," said Gary, "since it's here in the state. Then we can come home on the weekends."

As it turned out, however, after all the talk and excitement about what the three friends were looking forward to, Dwayne and Roy failed the physical examination and were refused admittance to the army, leaving Gary all alone to face the unknown.

Completing the final step in the enlistment process meant that Gary was officially considered government property. All that was left was the finalization of the paperwork that had to be completed before he left for home to inform his mother what he had done. So as he waited, he wandered the halls of the Custom House in somewhat of a daze, thinking about the decision he had just made, when he began feeling an emptiness in his gut the way in which one feels "buyer's remorse" after committing to a decision of a grand scale. Gary could hardly believe what had just happened. Only hours earlier he and his friends, Dwayne and Roy, were planning, what they thought, would be an exciting adventure of their life together under the army's "Buddy Program." *Yeah, so much for the buddy plan,* Gary thought. *Now I'm here on my own and I'm feeling sick about it.*

As Gary continued waiting for the paperwork to be done, he happened to pass by one of the offices in the building when he heard a voice calling out to him, saying, "Hey, young man, why are you wandering around the halls? Are you lost? You've passed by my office several times now. Come on in and have a seat," said the man, sitting behind a desk and dressed in a green uniform with medals pinned to his chest, several yellow stripes on the side of each arm, and hash marks slanted on the sleeve of his left arm. "I'm Sergeant Arness. I'm the army recruiter. And you are?"

"I'm Gary Trujillo."

"Are you joining up, Gary?" the sergeant asked.

"I already did," Gary said in a sorry sort of way. "I joined for two years under the voluntary draft."

"You did what?" the sergeant said in a high-pitched voice. Then: "Why on earth would you do that?"

"I volunteered for the draft because I didn't want to stay for three years. I figured two years was all that was required to fulfill my military obligation."

"Well, that's the dumbest thing I ever heard," barked the sergeant. "Now you're stuck for two years in some shithole cleaning latrines, working in the mess hall doing dishes, pulling guard duty, and all other kinds of crappy stuff, while those who enlisted in the regular army are given desk jobs and other kinds of cushiony positions."

The sergeant went on to explain further the difference between volunteering for two years and enlisting for three years. "Let me tell you," he continued, "if you had enlisted under regular army status, you would have been able to choose anywhere in the world to be stationed. Also, you could have chosen any area of training you wanted. You hear what I'm saying? You would have been able to tell the army what you wanted as an RA. Now the army is going to tell you what it wants you to do as a draftee. Do you understand what I'm trying to tell you?" the sergeant went on to exaggerate his point. "You do not have any say as to what you want for the next two years. The army's got you by the balls, and there's nothing you can do about it. Oh, and one other thing, every RA soldier you come in contact with while you're cleaning latrines will tease and harass the hell out of you to no end. Man! I can't believe you did such an asinine thing. You are in deep shit, my friend."

"Well, is there anything I can do? Can I change to regular army?" Gary asked somewhat startled.

"Hell, I don't know, it might be too late to do anything about it. Once someone commits to doing something, like you just did, it's pretty damn hard to reverse that decision. But let me make a few calls, maybe, just maybe, there is a way out, but no promises."

For the next few minutes Gary sat there, facing Sergeant Arness, thinking to himself, *Man, I really screwed up. I'm such a dummy for not finding out sooner the difference between RA and the draft status. Here I thought I was gonna be able to travel and see the world and learn a trade in the process. I sure hope I can change to regular army.* Just then, before Gary could continue berating himself, he heard the sergeant talking to someone on the telephone.

"Hey, Joe, Arness here, how goes it? That's great! When did the promotion go through? Well, congratulations! No, I'm still waiting for mine. Hopefully it won't be too long; I just need a couple of more . . . you know. So the reason I called, I have this young man in my office who, you would not believe what he did. Listen to this. He volunteered for the draft instead of regular army. Can you believe how crazy that was? Yeah! That's what I told him. Well, anyway, the damage is done. Unless of course, and that's why I called, there is some way out where he could change his status to regular army. There's not, huh?"

Just then, Gary could hear his heart pounding and the sick feeling he felt earlier increased. *Damn, what did I do,* he continued berating himself, *how could I have been so stupid, I should have talked to someone before making such a dumb decision.*

"What's that again, Joe? There may be a way? Okay, I'll wait for your call. And thanks."

Looking Gary straight in the eyes, Sergeant Arness echoed out, "Young man! You just may be the luckiest son of a b---- I've ever met. My friend, Sergeant Prescott, out of Washington, DC, with whom I entered the army under the army's Buddy Program twenty years ago, is going to see if he could pull a few strings and get your draftee status reversed to regular army. Understand this, though: this is highly unusual and has never been done before. So if you're a godly person, you better start praying. I'll be back in a sec. So just sit there and hope the hell he's successful. Here, take this pamphlet and read all about the great benefits the army offers, that is, if you're regular army."

Ten minutes later, just as Sergeant Arness walked back into his office, the telephone rang. "Sergeant Arness here, may I help you? Joe, that was fast. What did you find out? Yeah, okay. Anything else? You sure? Because I got the young man here in my office, sitting on pins and needles. Wow! That was easier than I thought. Well, thank you, my friend. I surely do appreciate your help. Now if he'll only agree, this may do it for me," Sergeant Arness said in a lower voice so as not to let Gary hear this last part of his conversation. "Thanks again, Joe."

"Am I going to be able to change my status?" Gary asked.

"Yes and no," Sergeant Arness answered.

"What does that mean? What happened?" asked Gary.

"It means, the only way I can make it happen is if you agree to authorize me to make the change, today, by recruiting you into the regular army. And, this is the best part, I can guarantee that you will be stationed anywhere in the world you chose once you finish your basic training here in the States. But I have to know now. Otherwise, if you wait any longer than today, you're stuck with the decision you made and no telling where you will be sent. So, are you willing to sign up today under regular army regulations? And if so, where would you like to be stationed after basic training?"

"I want to go to Europe. Maybe Spain or Germany," Gary said excitedly.

"Well then, okay. Let's get it over with, just in case something unexpected happens," Sergeant Arness said, just as excited as Gary, as if just pulling in a huge marlin.

"The rest is history," as they say. Gary changed his military status with the stroke of a pen and committed himself to three years, instead of two, of military service, and within two weeks was headed to Fort Leonard Wood, Missouri, where he spent his first week of military experience undergoing a major transformation from civilian to military life. This is what the army referred to as "Zero Week," in that it did not count toward the eight weeks of basic training. It was during this time that not only were heads shaved and new clothing issued (uniforms), but one's identity is stripped to the core; a different lifestyle and philosophy are induced through indoctrination and discipline; and loyalty and honor toward one's brotherhood and country are demanded as the foundation for survival.

It was a rude awakening that first week for Gary. All he could think was *Did I make a mistake by joining the army and adding that extra year to my enlistment?* That sick feeling he felt in his gut returned again, and in fact increased because of his homesickness, something he had never experienced before in his life. Never mind the daytime marching in 110 degree heat and humidity, the long hours of indoctrination classes, the long chow lines, the evening curfew, the early bedtime hours, or the nightly fire-watch duty, it was the nagging of this regretted decision and the homesickness that were the most bothersome for Gary to cope with.

Following that miserable experience of living in World War II barracks and suffering under the scorching heat during Zero Week, Gary was on his way to Fort Knox, Kentucky, to begin his eight weeks of basic training, where he would learn the fundamentals of handling weapons, hand-to-hand combat, nighttime maneuver fighting and survival techniques, and where he would take a series of battery tests to determine what he was best suited for in order to fulfill the army's critical job needs.

Basic training was another life-changing element Gary would undergo. The severe homesickness and regrets about joining the army he experienced earlier were slowly subsiding. There now was a structure in place for him to follow and virtually no time to think about home or anything else. For the next eight weeks his every move was dictated by the army as to when, where, and what he ate, when and where he slept, where he worked, and when extracurricular activities would be allowed. There was very little free time for extracurricular activities, given the stringently scheduled mandatory training and daily and nightly work detail assignments. In fact, when work details were assigned, Gary had observed that most of the daily and nightly work detailing, such as latrine, barracks, kitchen, and grounds cleanup, including guard duty, were performed mostly by regular army enlistees while draftees were assigned clerical office jobs, delivering mail and doing other soft jobs such as running errands and chauffeuring high-ranking officers to and fro. This pattern of treatment was also evident throughout Gary's time in the service, which was totally contrary to how the army recruiter had described the differing roles of draftees and regular army enlistees.

However, it all made sense, Gary rationalized years later. Just think about it, the average soldier of draft status was in their early twenties; many had college degrees and were, for the most part, mature adults. The draftees may have had significant work experience compared to the average RA teenager, freshly out of high school, with little or no work experience, wet behind the ears, if you will, immature in many ways, and perhaps with no future plans in sight. So it stands to reason, those with more life experiences were preferred over others who were just getting their "feet wet" to be given more responsibility and treated differently.

What made it easier, mentally and emotionally for Gary, was accepting his situation and then building camaraderie with new friends with whom he cultivated relationships. Given the circumstances under which military personnel are subjected, strong relationships are formed and develop into lasting friendships, regardless of racial backgrounds and personality traits.

After basic training, Gary remained at Fort Knox, in Kentucky, for two more months and attended Radio School, where he was trained in Morse code. *I guess this is what those battery of tests showed I would be best suited for and what the army is in need of based on how many of us are here,* he thought. By the end of the year

(1962), Gary was on his way to Germany, where he spent the remaining two and half years of his enlistment. He was first stationed in Dachau, the first concentration camp under Nazi Germany during World War II, where he and his three roommates operated as Morse code operators responsible for maintaining communications with other army posts throughout Europe. Several months later, without any prior notice, Gary was transferred to another army base in Germany, Schwabisch Gmünd, where he continued as a Morse code operator.

It wasn't long after arriving at his new location that Gary was approached by his company commander and asked if he would be willing to change his MOS (military occupation specialty code); his MOS was considered critical and required his signature to effect the change; it could not be arbitrarily changed by high command. It was explained that the current headquarters clerk, a draftee, would soon be ending his two years of service and that a replacement was needed to fill his position. And, so, from that point on until his separation from active duty (June 1965), Gary served as the headquarters clerk, which entailed multiple clerical and administrative responsibilities, such as preparing temporary travel orders; basic bookkeeping; maintaining headquarter records; cutting travel, promotion, and separation orders; and a host of other clerical functions. The most exciting moment of Gary's career in the army was when he cut his own separation orders and within thirty days was aboard a navy ship headed for home.

It had been two years, eleven months, and twenty-seven days since that unforgettable day that Gary and his friends, Dwayne and Roy, walked into the Custom House to join the army under the "Buddy Program," hoping to spend the next two years traveling the world together. Gary had learned later that his two friends, after failing their physical examination in Denver, had driven to New Mexico, where they enlisted and were accepted into the army there, serving three years, stateside, as paratroopers.

Moving Forward
chapter seven

Transitioning back into civilian life didn't take Gary too long. By the end of summer, after returning home, one of his childhood classmates, John, who had also recently ended his service with the army, helped him get a job at an oil company, working as a mail clerk handing out mail to chemists, engineers, and other highly educated individuals who held advanced degrees in other disciplines. One such individual was Gary's immediate supervisor, Stan, who said to him, "I want to encourage you to take advantage of the company's college tuition aid program. As long as you maintain a passing grade, the company will pay for your tuition. I don't care if you take basket weaving, you should strongly consider enrolling in college. Yes, it may take you a while to get a degree going part-time, but in the long run it's all worth it. You'll see."

Gary had recently been married to his high school sweetheart, whom he had known since the ninth grade. He did not take advantage of the company's tuition aid program that first year on the job, though the idea of furthering his education was constantly on his mind, coupled with the fact that other employees, including his friend, John, who were taking evening college classes served as motivating factors and reminders of the importance of working toward one's personal growth and development. So by the end of 1967, after Gary and his wife had the first of their three sons, Eric, he reluctantly submitted a college application to the University of Colorado, Denver, but was somewhat doubtful he'd be accepted given that his overall GPA while in high school was barely above 2.0. As it turned out, however, he was accepted but on a probationary basis until such time he completed remedial math and English courses required of all students entering college for the first time who do not meet the prerequisites for college-level classes.

Over the next year, while attending college in the evening and still working in the mail room, after his friend, John, had been promoted to a technician position, working with chemists, Gary had become frustrated and doubtful as to his future with the company. The frustration grew to the point where he didn't see any possible promotional opportunities and felt he could do better working elsewhere. His attitude was *If you can't move up, you have to move on.* And so he did, even though he didn't have another job waiting for him.

The next few months after leaving the oil company didn't give Gary any comfort, and his future seemed bleak, to say the least. He had jumped from one job to another, trying desperately to find that perfect work that would put him on the path to success. He first worked at a mattress company, followed by a suitcase manufacturer, a sports equipment wholesaler, and an electroplating plant, where he was fired because the company said he was dissatisfied with the working conditions. But Gary knew his dismissal was because he tried to intercede on behalf of an elderly co-worker who had limited physical dexterity, which caused him severe back pain, by asking their supervisor if he would allow the employee an extra morning and afternoon work break due to his condition. It was during the Vietnam War and the job entailed hanging small missile warheads on a rack to be electroplated, which required standing for long periods of time in one spot. A week later, Gary, once again, found himself looking for another job.

That year did not turn out as he had expected it would, in terms of moving up in the world. There was one bright light still shining on Gary's future, that of earning a college degree. With the help of the GI Bill, he had never stopped taking evening college courses since leaving the oil company. He knew that furthering his education was key to a brighter future and was determined to work toward that end.

As Gary continued his job search, which would eventually place him on the right path to success, reality set in. He had finally realized he'd made a grave mistake by leaving the oil company and regretted, deeply, having done so. He then conveyed his frustrations to his friend, John, who encouraged him to talk to Stan, his former supervisor, to see if the company would rehire him. So after swallowing his pride, Gary humbly asked to return and once again was delivering mail to all the employees.

It wasn't long after returning to the oil company that

Gary was promoted to the Reproduction Department, where he learned to operate the printing presses and process photographic materials for use by the biologist and other staffers. From that point on and for the next two years, Gary enjoyed working among the many highly educated scientists and professional administrators. He had, once again, established himself as a responsible, hardworking employee with an eagerness to do well and learn more while taking full advantage of studying in the company's library during his spare time. As well, Gary was highly thought of by his co-workers and management. Overall, working for the oil company was a positive and enriching experience for Gary, to have had the opportunity to contribute in an environment that both inspired and motivated him to develop into a more mature adult.

Toward the end of the 1960s and into the '70s, the country was embroiled in a social revolution for civil rights. People of color and other minorities, for decades, were treated as second-class citizens and subjected to disparate treatment and racial discrimination in education, housing, and employment. The government under President Johnson's "Great Society / War on Poverty" attempted to address these practices by establishing programs aimed toward helping economically and socially disadvantaged individuals from low-income areas, who had been suffering from the effects of poverty and discrimination. It was during this time that Gary learned of an educational program designed to address the educational needs of adults, by offering college-level courses on weekends and in the evenings. Although the program was administered by a four-year state college, a committee made up of five individuals, active in the community, was designated to hire resident counselors and provide oversight of the program's operations. As such, a search was held for counselors to conduct outreach recruitment of potential students, living in low-income, designated as "target," areas around the city, and to provide academic counseling services.

This educational concept intrigued Gary since he had once fit the profile the program was intended to serve and had been attending evening college part-time for the past four years. So in his mind he was the perfect match to be a resident counselor, helping others achieve their educational aspirations, and therefore he was convinced he was the ideal candidate for the job. Gary did not want to leave his position at that time, worried that others may think he was ungrateful, since he had been given a second chance to work for the company, so he discussed his interest in the college program with his supervisor, Stan, and his friend, John, who after all was instrumental in getting him the job at the oil company on both occasions. John and Stan were very supportive of him and had no doubt he "fit the bill" for the position. However, they were concerned that leaving a stable job with promotional opportunities for a position funded by federal funds (soft money) would in time fizzle out, given the nature of government programs. They felt that he was taking a big risk and ought to consider what he would be leaving. Gary was appreciative of their concerns and assured them he was mindful of the risk, but that this was something he knew he had to pursue, should he be selected. Gary then expressed his gratefulness for their help and confidence in him and assured them that his leaving, should he get the job, would not be as foolish a departure as it was the first time.

Several weeks had passed since Gary applied for one of the four resident counselor positions when he was notified that the hiring process was being delayed due to unforeseen circumstances. Doubt then began to set in and was a reminder of what was conveyed to him earlier, that he was taking a big risk leaving to work in a government program. Finally it happened, after waiting nearly two months: Gary was notified by the hiring board to come in for an interview.

What followed next was waiting and more waiting. Gary felt he had done well in the interview and was confident of his chances of being hired for one of the counselor positions. The way in which the program was described struck a chord with Gary. Since he was once one of those individuals the program was intended to help, he instinctively knew what it was going to take to perform the role of a counselor. And the fact that he was still working toward earning a college degree would come into play when it came time to provide academic counseling. Thus his background would be the influencing factor that would assure his being hired. It was as though the counselor's job description had been written just for him.

Several more weeks passed and still no response from the board. Then, after two and a half months since submitting his application, Gary received notification he had been hired for one of the resident counselor positions and the appointment would become effective in thirty days. Gary was elated by the news and immediately gave notice he would soon be leaving the oil company, once again. This had been Gary's first permanent job since separating from the army, and he was most grateful for the way in which he had been treated and for the trust placed in him by the company. Earlier on he was of a different mind-set and his immaturity had clouded his thinking.

The author, Gary, teaching a student.

Changing jobs once again was not something Gary hadn't already experienced, given the many jobs he'd held over the past several years, but the job he was now embarking upon, at the age of twenty-six, was different. The job was about not only providing a livelihood for him and his family but also helping others prepare for a brighter future by furthering their education, the same as he had been doing for the past four years. So over the next two years, in addition to canvassing "target area" communities, of which he himself was a product, for program participants, Gary conducted client orientations, personal counseling in a general sense, and academic advising. He also tutored students from time to time that were having difficulties in math, a subject he enjoyed.

Working those two years as an outreach college recruiter and advisor, under the auspices of a four-year college, helping students realize their educational dreams was the most rewarding and beneficial job Gary had yet experienced. In many ways he viewed it as a vocation, something he was called to do, rather than just another job. Helping the disadvantaged achieve upward mobility motivated him even more to continue his own educational pursuits.

While working for what was considered a "poverty program" during the years 1970 through 1972, Gary learned of other federally funded programs established under the "War on Poverty" era. One such program dealt with placing high school students into colleges and other postsecondary educational institutions throughout the state upon their graduation and helping them qualify for financial aid assistance. The program was similar in intent to what Gary was already involved in, and it piqued his interest because of its capacity to reach out to multitudes of Mexican American and other minority and disadvantaged students from several of the inner-city high schools. The program was under the direction of a national Mexican American organization essentially designed to provide employment training and job placement of low-income and unskilled Latinos. Each of these components, employment and education, was managed by program directors who, on a monthly basis, reported to a board of directors made up of fifteen members of the Hispanic community, representing grassroots organizations and the private and federal sectors. Also inherent in the structure of federally funded programs was oversight by the federal government regarding program compliance and the use of taxpayers' money.

As Gary learned more about the student college placement program, it turned out that the director was leaving for a position with the federal government and a new director was needed to fill his position. So because of Gary's experience and exposure working in a similar educational program and his ties with the Chicano community, he was encouraged to apply for the program directorship; within a month's time he was selected for the position. This was a giant step up in responsibility for Gary. The job required the supervision of several outreach counselors, who would spend most of their day stationed in inner-city high schools, talking to a large segment of low-income disadvantaged students and encouraging them to pursue a higher education, then helping them in the process with their admissions and financial aid applications. In essence, the program served as an adjunct to the school's internal counseling and guidance system and was coordinated with the state's superintendent of high schools, so as not to cause any disruptions within the school's operations. Further responsibilities involved administrative and budgetary matters regarding the program's continual funding and assurances that student services remained consistent with congressional intent.

Over the next two and a half years (March 1972–September 1974), the time and effort put forth by Gary and his staff resulted in placing large numbers of high school students in colleges and universities and other postsecondary educational institutions throughout the state of Colorado. Otherwise, these students may not have had the opportunity to pursue a higher education beyond the high school level. Also, in some incidences, students who had dropped out of high school were encouraged to enroll in GED (general equivalency diploma) programs, and then later helped toward pursuing other avenues of higher education.

Given the nature of certain entities, be they privately or government funded, governed by a large body of individuals of various political persuasions, the board Gary reported to was no exception. Of the fifteen members, seven represented one Mexican American organization and seven represented another Mexican American organization, while the last member, at various times, came from either organization. Even though both community groups worked toward the advancement of Mexican Americans/Chicanos/Latinos/Hispanics, their methods were not always the same nor were their philosophies or politics. Some were of a conservative bent, some liberal, and some in between, whose politics, over time, flowed over into the program operations, causing division and dissension among management and subordinates. As for Gary, his only concerns were helping high school students reach their educational potential and defending the integrity of the program by not allowing the political atmosphere taint his views nor disrupt how the program was managed. As hard as he tried, however, Gary soon found himself embroiled in the organization's politics after taking issue with a certain board member's attempt to interfere with a decision Gary made regarding one of his counseling staff. After several attempts made to the board of directors to intervene on his behalf, it became apparent that the politics overshadowed the interests of the program, thus his plea to the board to help resolve the issue at hand was never adequately addressed and the interference and harassment continued. In fact, the interfering board member even went as far as accusing Gary of purchasing a life insurance policy for personal use, which he was compelled to defend himself against, with the help of a friend who was a lawyer, since the policy was purchased on behalf of his staff. Again, the board of directors chose not to come to Gary's defense. One board member even said to Gary, "You have to become political." It wasn't long after that Gary resigned.

Again, Gary made a decision to resign from a job without the assurance of another job to fall back on, something he vowed he'd never do again. "What were you thinking?" "How are you going to support the family?" "Are you crazy?" were the questions family and friends fired at him. The one thing Gary had going for him, though, was that he was close to earning enough credits to complete his degree; then he would be set, jobwise, so he thought. The year was 1975 and Gary had continuously taken classes, either on a full-time or a part-time basis, since first enrolling in college in 1966, when he worked at the oil company.

For the next several months, Gary managed to support his family by teaching a class at one of the community colleges, a course he designed, which was geared toward helping first-time students adjust to the college environment: "Everything You Ever Wanted to Know about College but Were Afraid to Ask." Gary was also receiving monthly stipends under the GI Bill for educational expenses and, periodically, performed various tasks for a community-based health program. By midyear 1976, after going to college for the past ten years, Gary finally graduated with a bachelor's degree majoring in psychology and minoring in business administration.

Then something unexpected happened. Gary was visiting a friend who worked at the college he had recently graduated from, when a college professor from a major university in Washington State, who was in town visiting family, happened to stop by to inquire if there were any recent Chicano/Latino college graduates interested in attending graduate school. Gary chimed in on the conversation and said he had just completed his degree but hadn't given any thought to continuing his education; after ten years of working toward his degree, he felt he needed to find suitable employment to support his family. At which point, the professor indicated that the university, where he taught architecture, was expanding its recruitment efforts toward minority students and was offering scholarships and financial aid in the form of work study, loans, and grants. The professor went on, further describing the university and the opportunities it offered to both graduate and undergraduate minority students; it was one of a few major universities in the country actively involved in minority recruitment.

The concept of graduate school sparked an interest in Gary, especially when the professor mentioned that the director of financial aid was a person with whom Gary was familiar; they had met while placing high school students in colleges throughout the state of Colorado.

That person had been the financial aid director at one of those colleges. So Gary called that individual to inquire about what type of financial aid package he would be eligible for should he decide to apply to the university. Gary also expressed his interest in higher education administration and wanted to know if the university offered a master's degree in the subject. He asked what the campus was like and how was living in Seattle. Gary was pleased to hear that the university's College of Education did offer a master's degree in education, which was only a one-year program. He would need to apply as soon as possible since the fall quarter was only a few months away.

Upon returning home that day, and somewhat excited about the possibility of going to graduate school, Gary announced to his wife, "Pack the bags, we are moving to Seattle, Washington. I'm going to graduate school to work on my master's degree in education, which is only a one-year program and then we can return to Colorado."

"You've got to be kidding," his wife said. "You just finished getting your degree. After how many years? Oh yeah, fifty!" she said somewhat sarcastically. "Don't you think it's time you started looking for a job? What on earth are you thinking? It's one thing for you and me to just pick up and leave, but, if you haven't noticed, we have three young boys, one of whom is only two years old, not to mention we're barely making it financially. How do you think we're going to live?"

It had been seven months since Gary last held a full-time job, and their finances were slowly dwindling.

And the monthly stipend he had been receiving under the GI Bill had terminated now that he had graduated from college. The only source of income coming in was from his part-time teaching at the community college. Also, his wife Nancy's parents had been a tremendous help when things got rough financially. At that moment reality set in, causing Gary to ponder what he had been putting his family through over the past several years, going from one job to another, either by choice or unforeseen circumstances, never establishing any roots. The only consistent thing Gary had stuck to was staying in college. He knew in his heart that eventually his dream for a comfortable life for him and his family would become a reality, so he couldn't give in and needed to stay focused, convinced that persistence would pay off and the hardship they were experiencing would end.

Over the next several days, Gary and his wife had further discussions about what more they would have to endure if he were to spend another year in school, instead of searching for that ideal job in higher education he had hoped to obtain. While it was a challenge trying to convince his wife that getting a master's degree would enhance his chances toward achieving his goal, she reluctantly agreed and the planning began. First, there was the matter of selling their house, which in hindsight was a poor decision on Gary's part. Second, a place to live in Seattle had to be secured, which meant that Gary would need to drive to Seattle, find a house to rent, leave his vehicle, fly back home, rent a large enough truck to hold eight rooms of furniture, load the truck, then drive it back to Seattle, all of which occurred within two months. Gary's wife and their three sons, Donald (age two), Christopher (age seven), and Eric (age nine), joined him a week later, and for the remainder of that summer did a lot of sightseeing and experienced the beauty of the Evergreen State before the school year began.

Though Gary had been accepted by the university, the College of Education had not yet officially accepted him. It turned out he did not do well in his graduate school entrance exams but was admitted on a probationary basis and allowed to enroll in classes to begin his program until such time he demonstrated academic proficiency, meaning he had to maintain a B average. By the end of the school year, Gary had completed his studies, earning him a master's of education degree. Interestingly, during the school year, Gary had still not been notified whether he had been accepted into the College of Education, though his grade point average was well above a B. It wasn't until after he graduated that the College officially notified him of his acceptance.

Gary knew at the outset he had to do well in his studies and would not accept rejection after uprooting his family, selling their house, and moving fourteen hundred miles away from family and friends. The first few months living in Seattle were lonely for the Trujillos. While Gary struggled with his studies, the kids went to school. With a lack of finances, the family spent what free time they had visiting the zoo, walking around Green Lake, and from time to time visiting with other Chicano/Latino graduate students who, with their families, had also migrated to Seattle from other parts of the country to obtain their advanced degrees in dentistry, law, education, health administration, and other professional disciplines.

By January 1977, Gary and his wife had made a down payment on a house with the proceeds from the sale of their first house. The house they purchased was near the schools and close to the freeway, giving Gary easy access when commuting to the university. It was always Gary's intention to return to Denver once he obtained his master's degree, so buying a house in Seattle was an investment toward that end. The year passed and the plan to return to Colorado was under way. The second house was sold within a couple of weeks. Gary's wife's parents and grandparents drove to Seattle in their RV to help with the move, and by the end of summer 1977, the family was headed back to the Southwest.

The plan, once they arrived in Denver, was to stay with Gary's mother until such time he purchased another house and secured permanent employment. Gary thought that earning a master's degree in education administration would guarantee him a job in one of the community colleges or four-year colleges, where he would eventually establish a professional career in higher education and live "happily ever after." As he soon found out, however, this was wishful thinking. Over the next year Gary struggled day by day, searching for a position throughout the college system, without ever once being granted an interview. Though there were several positions he could have qualified for, based on his experience and educational background, given the opportunity.

As the months passed, the family's temporary living

arrangement became a strain on both the family and Gary's mother, who had taken them in and tried making their stay as comfortable as possible, given the limited space in the house Gary and his wife had purchased for her a few years back. Though his mother's house was small, so were Gary and Nancy's three young sons, who slept on two couches in the living room, while the couple slept in one of the two bedrooms.

As the months rolled by, frustration and depression took hold of Gary, causing him to ask himself, time and time again, *Am I ever going to achieve my hopes and dreams of becoming a college administrator, or am I going to end up in some dead-end job punching a time clock? I don't want the past eleven years going to college day and night to be in vain. I've worked too hard, and my family has sacrificed too much for me to fail them.*

Being out of meaningful work for nearly three years was causing Gary to begin losing confidence in his abilities. He started questioning himself as to whether he possessed the necessary skills to compete in a highly competitive educational environment, though he knew he couldn't give up trying. It had been a long journey since he began taking evening college classes and working with adults and high school students to help them achieve their academic potential. Now it was his time to move further along in the journey to success, which he'd worked so hard on. So for the sake of his family, he had to continue searching for that ideal job within the educational system, commensurate with his work experience and educational background. He had sacrificed too much to give up now.

The Call

chapter eight

Several months had passed and still no job leads. Gary was growing more and more apprehensive about his future. The only thing that kept him from finally throwing in the towel was his wife, who never gave up hope of her husband's abilities and passion to succeed. She was always in his corner, prompting him to continue what he started. Although at times, because of Gary's frustrations, and anxieties due to his situation, there were moments of tension between him and his wife.

Then the unexpected happened. After living with his mother close to a year, Gary received a call from the University of Washington. The caller was Gary's friend, the financial aid officer, who was aware of his dilemma, informing him that a position had opened up within the Minority Affairs department. The position was director of the Chicano Student Services division, which was one of several ethnic student service programs on campus, the others being for black, Asian, Native American, and disadvantaged white students, designed to recruit and provide counseling services to both minority and nonminority students from socially and economically disadvantaged backgrounds. The university was noted, throughout the country, for its strong advocacy of the recruitment of minority graduate and undergraduate students under its Affirmative Action program. This was right up Gary's alley. He was excited about applying for the director's position and in some way had been longing to move back to Washington State after experiencing so many disappointments and hardships since returning home a year earlier. Although his wife didn't necessarily want to move back again, she knew this was what her husband needed to recover from what was becoming chronic depression. And while, deep down, Gary would have rather stayed in Denver, working in higher education, his current circumstances had become unbearable so, if offered the job, he couldn't pass it up. Too much time had passed being unemployed, and living under his mother's roof was unacceptable.

"Are we moving back to Seattle?" their eldest son, Eric, asked. "Can I go with you when you move the furniture?"

"We will see," Gary said. "First I have to apply for the job. I may not even get it."

"Yeah you will!" his son said.

After applying for the director's position, it took a few weeks for a response. Gary was one of three candidates called in for an interview, and so once again he was on his way to Seattle. Not knowing how long the process would take or what his chances were of being hired, he refrained from building up his hopes. After all, he was used to rejection and simply wanted to take everything in stride. Gary called a friend in Seattle to share the news and was invited to stay at his home while in town. The visit was short, the interview over, and after three days there Gary was on his way back to Denver, without any clue as to how the interview went. Upon returning home, two weeks had passed and still no response from the university. Then doubt began to set in. "I guess I didn't get the job," he told Nancy. "Now what am I going to do?"

"What is the saying?" his wife asked rhetorically. "No news is good news."

Finally, the wait was over. Gary was in the backyard of his mother's house, cleaning the porch, when his wife called out: "Garr, the mail just arrived and you got a letter from the university!"

"It's probably another rejection," he said as he stopped what he was doing and entered the house.

"Don't be so damn negative," his wife said with a somewhat angry tone in her voice. "It's not only about you, you know. What do you think the kids and I have been going through these past couple of years? It hasn't exactly been a picnic. So just open the damn letter and stop your whining."

"Yeah, you're right and I'm so sorry. You've been nothing but patient and understanding all this time. And, while I don't show it, I'm really appreciative."

"Okay, okay, hurry up and let's find out what's in store for us," his wife said excitedly.

As Gary carefully opened the envelope and then took out the letter and unfolded it, the word "CONGRATULATIONS!" jumped out at him, and in that moment, he felt a sense of relief flowing throughout his whole body. The heavy burden he had been carrying around with him since moving in with his mother suddenly dissipated. He had been selected as the director of the Chicano Student Services division at one of the most prestigious universities in the country. He had achieved his goal of becoming a college administrator. Now he could start building a career in higher education.

Shortly after receiving the good news, Gary got a clipping of an article from the university's student newspaper the *Daily*. It read, "Today the acting vice president for Minority Affairs announced the hiring of Denver native Gary Trujillo to the position of director of the Chicano Student Services division." The director's position had been vacant for nearly ten months following the departure of its former director, who was part of a massive student movement protesting against the university's lack of Chicano and other minority student enrollment.

"Wow! I'm impressed, Dad. See, I told you, you would get the job," Eric reminded him. "Now I can drive back with you."

"No, Eric, not until I find a place for us to live. Besides, I have to start my job in a couple of weeks and you and Christopher will still be in school. Once I do find a place, though, I'll return home, and by that time you'll be out of school. Then I'll rent a U-Haul truck and you can drive back with me."

By mid-April 1978, everything seemed to be falling into place. Gary was working again, this time for a major university, in a field in which he felt most comfortable and was well qualified, where he would be working again with Chicano and other Hispanic students, helping them achieve their educational potential. *It all paid off,* he thought, *the experience gained working for those poverty programs, never once giving up on my desire to earn a college degree that took ten years to accomplish, and taking a chance moving across the country to another state, family and all, to earn an advanced degree, though the journey was hard and very scary at times. Now no more waking up in the middle of the night and wondering how we are going to make it, financially, and whether I'll be able to provide a livelihood for my family. What a relief. It feels so good!*

At the time Gary was starting his new job, a controversial issue had taken over campus, which had begun when he was in graduate school there but he hadn't given it much thought due to his studies and work-study job in the financial aid office. Since then, the issue had escalated and student demonstrations had grown. The issue had to do with the firing of a Chicana secretary by her supervisor, also of Mexican descent, a tenured professor. So when Gary arrived on campus, Chicano students, along with some Chicano community activists, were protesting the firing. In a way this brought back memories of when he himself was faced with a similar situation, three years earlier, when he held the directorship of a poverty program and was falsely accused of mismanagement by a member of his board of directors, which was the impetus for resigning from his position. So he understood the political ramifications and remained neutral.

What Gary didn't know, on his first day in the office, was how politicized the issue had become nor was he aware that two of his counseling staff were actively involved, in support of the secretary, who didn't seem to care they were neglecting their student counseling responsibilities by continually taking part in the demonstrations during working hours.

By mid-morning an all-hands staff meeting of the entire department was called by the acting vice president to introduce and welcome Gary as the new director of the Chicano Student Services division. In all, Gary was in the company of thirty staff members, including the directors of the other four ethnic student divisions. However, visibly absent were the two counselors Gary had been briefed on by his immediate supervisor regarding their political agenda. Also, it was widely known throughout the student divisions who these individuals were and why they were not in attendance. All in all it was a pleasant welcoming and Gary felt good about his new environment.

Following the all-hands meeting, Gary called a meeting of his staff, consisting of a secretary and four student counselors, two of whom did not attend. As he was preparing for the meeting, he thought to himself, *How am I going to handle this? I've only been on the job a few hours and, already, I may have a potential employee problem that may get out of hand if not handled properly.* The meeting proceeded with the remaining two counselors and office secretary, who were friendly and cordial though somewhat guarded, which was understandable, given the political atmosphere and the department's choice for the directorship of the division.

Here, Gary was an inner-city Chicano outsider from

another state, who was hired over several Washington State Chicano candidates, some of whom had graduated from the UW, held master's degrees and strong ties with the Chicano community, and who themselves at one time worked in the fields with their parents and siblings, picking fruit and vegetables under poor environmental conditions, just like so many of the students in the Chicano division had done. So who better qualified to relate to these students and guide them through a major university housing over thirty-seven thousand students?

After a few back-and-forth pleasantries with the three staffers, Gary shared a little of his background and assured them that his only interest was seeing to it that the students in their division received the best counseling and guidance that would lead them to academic success; he understood fully the intent of the Minority Affairs department and its overall mission and why it existed in the first place. Gary went on, further, to explain his commitment to social causes with regard to helping minority and other disadvantaged individuals realize their potential. Gary knew why he was there, and in time it would become clear not only to his staff but to the students as well.

Just as the meeting was about to end, the other two counselors whom Gary had not yet met walked in and sat down at the table. One of the counselors, a male, seemed very friendly, though the other individual, a female, folded her arms and just stared at her new supervisor as if to say "Bring it on, *cabrón!*" There was no mistaking her body language; she was expressing an attitude of defiance. Gary thought, *Wow! This is going to be interesting. I guess before I start working on anything productive, I'm going to have to deal with some strong personalities.*

It wasn't the first time Gary was face-to-face with an employee that demonstrated, what appeared to be, a challenge toward management. He had encountered this type of dynamic personality when he'd directed the high school student college placement program. That time, however, the employee did not display such a brazen attitude as had the person sitting in front of him now. This time, Gary was banking on the support of higher management, something he didn't have back then, should a situation arise that forced him to take some sort of disciplinary action regarding infraction of the rules, insubordination, or some other inappropriate behavior deemed necessary to address.

The male counselor, on the other hand, was pleasant and respectful in the way in which he introduced himself and his co-worker since she hadn't spoken up. After spending a few more minutes reiterating his earlier discussion with the two latecomers, Gary convened the meeting and waited until they all left the room. As he sat there contemplating what he had just witnessed from the one female employee, his supervisor, one of the assistants to the VP, walked in and asked, "How did your meeting go with the staff?"

"For the most part, good," Gary answered. "Though I think it's going to be a challenge with one of them."

"You needn't say more. I know who you're talking about," said Gary's supervisor. "The department has had to deal with her now for several years. She's a real piece of work and a pain in the ass at that. If you know what I mean?"

Gary didn't feel comfortable as to where the conversation was going, so he tried to be positive about how he was going to focus on working with all his staff to remind them of what their responsibilities were and what the department's mission was. It didn't concern him what anyone's politics were as long as they were kept out of the office. He had a program to manage, and that was his only priority. The students came first and foremost. There was nothing more important than providing quality educational services to the students and ensuring that the integrity of the program remained intact.

A couple of weeks passed by and Gary was learning more about the politics that had engulfed the Chicano division to the point that many students stayed away for fear of being pressured into joining a Chicano student organization formed for the purpose of uniting Chicano students around various school functions, including activities associated with political issues. Though Gary was not against the organization, and in fact was fully supportive of its goals, he did not want students who were in the office for counseling services to be pressured or, in any way, intimidated by other students to join the organization. The office was not the place for this sort of activity. It was disruptive, and Gary was not going to condone such behavior; he made it very clear to his staff. Besides, the student organization, along with other ethnic student organizations, had its own office on campus grounds. Gary was not going to allow his office to be overtaken by any student group.

The time came, however, when the office policy was tested. The president of the student organization, an outspoken, charismatic, articulate, and extremely intelligent student, would stop by the office on a regular basis to visit with the rebellious female counselor and spend hours in her office, while other students were waiting to be served. While Gary allowed the visits to go unaddressed for a short period of time, he later confronted the student president, which at first was uncomfortable and somewhat combative, and thereafter that student would only stop by the office on occasion. Next, Gary confronted the counselor about the excessive time she was spending with the student president when she needed to exert more energy with her other students, who had greater counseling needs. Of course this didn't go over well with the counselor, who then became irate and indignant at the suggestion she wasn't doing her job well enough. The following month she resigned.

Two months had passed when another counselor resigned, stating he had secured a position working as an outreach counselor for a health clinic. He was the other counselor that had come in late to the meeting Gary held the first day on the job. It turns out he had recently earned his master's degree in health administration and was biding his time until an opportunity came up in the health field. Gary found out later from other staff members that this other counselor had also applied for the director's position. He had never made mention of it while under Gary's supervision and never displayed any resentment toward him. On the contrary, he was respectful, helpful, and accommodating. He was also well liked by the other counselors and the students.

As the weeks passed, normality within the office became standard. More students began making appointments to meet for counseling; it was becoming a heavy load for the two remaining counselors to serve them. This matter would not be addressed until such time that a new vice president was brought on board. In the meantime, Gary would fill in, allowing him to become more acquainted with the students and their needs.

As Gary was making arrangements to return to Denver to move his family and household goods back to Seattle, a second time, and after buying a house, sight unseen by his wife, there was still one last item on his agenda to fulfill. Each year the department held a student fund-raiser awards dinner to supplement its budget. During this celebration event a student in their last year of college from each of the student divisions is selected for their high academic marks and involvement in other curricular activities and then presented with a plaque describing their achievements. A tribute not only intended toward students but to the fund-raising board for their outreach in fund-raising efforts. Unbeknownst to Gary, the event was to occur three days before his departure, so when learning about it, he had a short time to understand more about the logistics.

It was the role of each division director to introduce their student and present them with a plaque, followed by a short presentation highlighting the student's accomplishments. While Gary was just getting over his recent encounters with one of his staff members and the student president of the Chicano student organization, an unexpected incident occurred during that evening of tribute. Earlier that week, Gary had met with the student to learn more about his story so that he could prepare a short bio and present it to the audience at the event. The meeting, he felt, went well, and he was pleased with the outcome. The student was cordial and open about his experiences while attending the university and seemed appreciative for having been chosen to be honored. Gary was now prepared to make his remarks.

The night of the awards dinner was filled with over three hundred guests, consisting of family and friends of the awardees, and strong supporters of the university's Minority Affairs program, who, over the years, had contributed greatly of their time and financial support. All in all, the event was a grand display of support toward the students made possible by the large number of financial contributors. Then there was a "hiccup" in what otherwise was a successful evening. After Gary introduced the Chicano division's choice for the Student of the Year Award, and presented him with a bronze-plated plaque inscribed with lettering of appreciation, the student proceeded to give a political speech about the lack of representation of Latino students and employees on campus and the university's failure to address the matter. Then the awardee said, "And when it does hire a Hispanic, it hires a person to direct the Chicano division who doesn't even speak Spanish." After which there was total silence throughout the entire dining room.

Though Gary was taken aback and surprised by the student's remark, after having met with him earlier that week and experiencing a pleasant meeting, he wasn't offended; he didn't take it personally since the student really knew nothing about him. Others in the audience, however, were embarrassed over the situation; some took offense but were discreet about their remarks. One of the Chicano faculty members, though, was irate over the student's remarks and said to Gary, "I'm going to bring this incident up at the next Chicano faculty meeting, maybe there's something we can do."

Gary replied, "No, Jim, there's no need to shed any more light on the matter. The student was given a platform and merely said what was on his mind, and he did. So please let it go."

"Well, the faculty is still going to hear about this," the professor mumbled as he walked away.

The fact that Gary didn't speak Spanish had only once been brought up in the past in relation to a job, and that was the time he directed the high school student recruitment program and reported to a board of directors, all of whom were Mexican Americans, as a function of his directorship. It was never made an issue with regard to his qualifications, perhaps due to the fact that the majority of the program's clients of Mexican descent were not bilingual.

As a Mexican American growing up in the inner city of Denver, not speaking Spanish was common for Gary's generation. Parents simply did not raise their children to carry on the language, generally speaking, that is. There were, of course, kids Gary grew up with who did speak the language, though not in public. Gary was of the notion that for his generation living in the inner city, speaking Spanish was not encouraged due to historic discrimination of Americans of Mexican descent. The fact is, Mexican Americans of Gary's parents' generation were publicly shamed for speaking Spanish outside the home and in the schools, which could account for many parents not passing on the language while raising their children in the inner city. They did not want them to experience the same humiliation caused by racial discrimination.

It wasn't until the civil rights movement in the late 1960s and '70s that one's ethnic heritage was displayed with honor—when speaking Spanish in public became an expression of pride by Mexican Americans; "black" was beautiful and no longer thought of as a derogatory term; the indigenous people, prior to the discovery of America, were actually Native Americans and not Indians as Columbus had called them, thinking he had discovered India; and other ethnic groups, such as Japanese, Chinese, and other Asian Americans, celebrated their love of their culture.

The following week Gary was on his way to Denver to arrange the move back to Seattle. He had purchased a house five miles from the university in a quiet neighborhood near both public and private schools, including a Catholic school, where all three of his sons would go. The house was in need of a lot of cosmetic repairs but had, what one friend said, "potential." Once again, Gary was able to buy the house from the proceeds he received from his younger brother, Paul, who bought the house that Gary and his wife had purchased for their mother several years back, on the condition she continue living in it.

Two weeks later, Gary and his eldest son, Eric, who

was ten years old at the time, drove back to the Pacific Northwest in a twenty-four-foot U-Hall truck loaded down with eight rooms of furniture, which had been stored in his brother's garage the entire year they lived with his mother. Soon after, his wife and two other sons, Christopher and Donald, ages eight and three, respectively, arrived in Seattle.

The year was 1978, and for the first time in three years, Gary felt a sense self-worth. He was now an administrator in higher education at a prestigious university, working in an environment he had longed to inhabit. He was making a livable salary for his family, they lived in a welcoming community, and more importantly they had the support of their family.

The following two years at the university were the most satisfying and enjoyable time Gary had since working as a college recruiter/counselor, helping adults continue their education, followed by directing and supervising the work of others engaged in helping high school students realize their dreams. Now as a credentialed administrator with an undergraduate degree in psychology and business administration and a master's degree in education with an emphasis in college administration, he once again was in a position to help Mexican American/Chicano/Latino students achieve their educational goals. Finally, all that Gary had worked for in the past fourteen years had paid off. He could go on now for the next thirty or so years, working in a field he was passionate about, which to him was more of a vocation than just a job, and then retiring in comfort.

Shortly after Gary's appointment, a new vice president

was hired to oversee the entire Minority Affairs office; he was also given tenure and a faculty position in the political science department. Gary and the other division directors participated in the hiring process in an advisory capacity and had an opportunity to provide their input in the selection process. While there were some negative feelings from some of the directors toward the candidate who ultimately was hired, Gary was extremely impressed by the way in which he had responded to the barrage of questions by the selection board and his ability to articulate the issues affecting minority students. In fact, after the candidate was selected to fill the VP position, Gary couldn't say enough positive things about him to other university faculty and staff. Of course not everyone, including his peers in the department, shared Gary's enthusiasm about the vice president and tried in subtle ways to persuade Gary to step back and take a "wait and see" position.

Given the history of the Minority Affairs office, in terms of how it came to be, the minority community was very much a part in its development and growth since the civil rights movement in the late 1960s. As such, Gary felt it was necessary to share what he thought of the new VP with members of the Chicano community leadership representing the various social organizations. Again, Gary was cautioned not to put too much stock in the university's selection of the new vice president but to focus more on what he would do to increase the enrollment and retention of minority students. The advice given was based on historical struggles between the minority community and the university that led up to the establishment of the Minority Affairs office, a history Gary could not ignore, nor would he, given his commitment to social justice. Ever since Gary's first encounter with the social programs, his philosophy was that he would defend the programs to the best of his ability if they were in danger of being harmed or subjected to dismantlement. He took this philosophy to heart, given the sacrifices made by many individuals fighting for social justice dating back to the mid 1960s.

Over the next two years (1978–80), Gary felt he was finally on a path that would secure his livelihood for the remainder of his professional career. He had accomplished his educational and employment goals, had a respectable position in higher education, and had established himself as a serious student advocate in a position to affect change with regard to helping Chicano/Latino students pursue their educational goals. And considered "icing on the cake" was the high praise and support given to Gary by the vice president for the way in which he managed the affairs of his division. Still others throughout the department remained suspicious of the new vice president. Then things started to unravel at the seams.

Unbeknownst to Gary, and perhaps because of his naivete, although the signs were apparent for others, the new VP was hired to implement significant changes to the admissions policy and to restructure how the student divisions functioned. For the next several weeks, there were daily meetings between the division directors and upper management to formulate a plan as to how changes were to be made. During the initial planning stage, Gary was on board and supportive of the VP, and continued giving him the benefit of the doubt that the "plan" being devised would complement student services and increase enrollment. The general feeling, though, among the other directors was that the VP was merely placating them in an effort to calm their suspicions. Then it became abundantly clear that the input by the directors was not taken seriously by upper management, at which point a strong resistance against any changes to the admissions policy by the division directors and their staff evolved. The very idea of changing the admissions policy was not an acceptable proposition. For too long universities throughout the country had admissions policies that systematically excluded many minority students from pursuing a higher education; it wasn't until the late 1960s, during the civil rights movement, that changes were made allowing a greater number of minority enrollments. As for the restructuring of the student divisions, although the preference among the staff was to remain as separate ethnic units, it wasn't as high a priority to resist that change as it was to resist changes to the admissions policy.

For the next several weeks, during the summer of 1980, resistance to the proposed changes to the admissions policy flowed over into the ethnic student organizations and then into the minority communities, whereby mass demonstrations developed campus-wide, protesting the implementation of any new changes to the existing admissions policy, which had been in place over ten years. There was also concern by some of the minority faculty that changing the admissions policy would, once again, curtail the enrollment of minority students, but they were reluctant to share their views publicly.

By midsummer the president of the university directed his vice provost and some of the minority faculty to meet with the organizers of the demonstration, made up of students and representatives of the minority community, to try and bring closure to the demonstrations by reaching some sort of mutual agreement—what the university referred to as negotiations. As it turned out, though, the meeting was one-sided. The university tried to explain the rationale for wanting to change the admissions policy based on the *Regents of the University of California v. Bakke* court decision, whereby a student named Allan Bakke sued the University of California for discrimination, for denying him admission to the medical school on the basis that he was white. The media referred to it as "reverse discrimination." The university stated it was merely taking a proactive approach for fear of a backlash of its admissions policy, with regard to minority students. Thus there was no intent by the university's representatives to negotiate in good faith. "It's all a sham," said one of the community representatives. "You guys don't want to negotiate, you want to dictate—something you're good at. The Bakke decision you reference is an overreaction by the university and doesn't even deserve to be given credibility. And yet the university is reacting by changing the admissions policy because a white student claims he was discriminated against because he's white. Really? Is that the university's rationale for wanting to change the admissions policy back to what it was? A policy that was found to be discriminatory against Latinos, blacks, and other minorities?" Nothing more was said and the meeting ended.

Needless to say, the protests escalated and got more vocal. More students and community supporters joined in, and the media coverage grew. An effigy of the vice president was burned down, symbolizing hatred toward the man who was brought in by the university to dismantle the Minority Affairs office. Following the massive campus demonstrations were two waves of arrests of demonstrators by campus police for refusing to leave the building housing the Minority Affairs, Admissions, and the Financial Aid Offices. In all, seventy-eight students, community supporters, and several staff members, including Gary, were arrested for trespassing. After their arrests, straws were drawn among those who owned property to see who would put up their home for collateral in order to obtain a bond. As it turned out, however, all seventy-eight protesters appeared in court the following day and were given one year deferred sentences and released from jail.

From that point on, the proposed changes to the admissions policy and the restructuring of the ethnic student divisions were put on hold. The demonstrations came to an end, but tension built throughout the department as if something was about to happen. And then something did. The vice president retaliated against those staff members that had participated in the demonstrations by denying cost of living raises, terminating a clerical staff member for what seemed a minor infraction of office policy, and suspending Gary for three days. In Gary's case, he had called in sick on a Friday morning and left a message with his secretary that he would not be coming into the office that day. An hour later he received a call from the office, whereby his five-year-old son, Donald, answered, "He's outside cutting the grass." Then the caller hung up. The following Monday morning as Gary entered his office, there was an envelope on his desk with a letter inside from the vice president, which read in part, "You are hereby suspended for three days without pay, to be effective immediately, for failing to properly inform the office of your absence . . ."

The action taken by the VP, in Gary's view, was retaliatory for his involvement in opposing the proposed admissions policy changes. Once again, Gary found himself in an untenable situation similar to what had happened several years back that precipitated his resignation from the educational program he'd directed under the auspices of the two Mexican American organizations. At that time, Gary had reprimanded one of his counselors for spending an enormous amount of time making long-distance personal phone calls and charging them to the office budget. Gary's actions toward this individual resulted in a false claim charged against him by one of the board of directors, who was close friends with the counselor in question, that he had purchased an insurance policy for his own personal gain. Such a charge was devastating to Gary, so he threatened to bring a lawsuit against the board of directors since they knew the claim was a fabrication but did nothing to intervene on his behalf. Behind the scene, one of the directors had conveyed to him his support and suggested Gary learn to play the "politics." The false claim was eventually dropped for fear of litigation and the potential of bad press. Needless to say, this too (the actions by the VP) did not go over well with Gary since it had been an established policy throughout the office, ever since he'd arrived on campus, that calling in sick and leaving a message with whomever took the call was routine.

What was once a close professional and personal relationship between Gary and the vice president had turned adversarial. The enthusiasm, self-assurance, and excitement Gary had exhibited when he'd first arrived on campus had now vanished. By the end of summer that same year (1980), the student division directors were reassigned to different positions and their directorships dissolved, leaving the ethnic student divisions to be supervised by one person. As for Gary, he was appointed to assist the assistant VP of budget and was moved to an office two doors down from the VP.

It wasn't long after that Gary was moved again, only this time off campus to a house converted into an office building. His office was in the basement behind the furnace room, where he would spend the next four and a half years away from the rest of the department's personnel. Though Gary had a title (assistant to the assistant VP of budgets), an office assistant, and a decent salary, he had no meaningful responsibilities. He simply reported to work every day, hoping things would change for the better over time, but that was not going to happen. He was isolated from the rest of his co-workers and ostracized from daily group-related functions. He had been humiliated by his vice president and became terribly frustrated over his situation.

By early 1985, four and a half years since the demonstrations had taken place, Gary's situation still hadn't changed and he felt that his skills were slowly rusting away. He was experiencing self-doubt and a lack of confidence about his abilities and so, as not to let his situation worsen, he looked into doing some part-time teaching at one of the local community colleges. Being that he had an advanced degree and related work experience, he was hired to teach a human relations (personnel) course, an introduction to business administration, and a business class titled "Wage and Salary Administration." Over the next few months, Gary's lack of self-esteem began to fade as he continued teaching. He now felt good about himself and was beginning to, as they say, "get back on the horse."

The summer of 1985 was coming to an end, and although Gary's self-worth had resurfaced through his teaching, he often thought about how it might have been had he not taken the UW position during that tumultuous year of 1980. His once-promising career in higher education administration at a prestigious university may never happen. Gary tried to put a positive spin on his thinking by not giving up. He was still bent on remaining in higher education as a career, though he knew it wasn't to be at the university.

What happened next was a total surprise. A Chicano faculty member visited Gary's office unexpectedly and conveyed to him in confidence that the university was willing to offer him a full year's salary if he would agree to resign within the next thirty days. (The university meaning the vice president.) The sound of a year's salary was enticing since Gary was no longer of significant value to his department nor had he been the past several years. He was simply someone whom upper management had put out to pasture. So that evening Gary discussed the university's offer with his wife and the decision was to accept it and move on with their life. It was not only hard for Gary, the past few years, reporting to work day after day, knowing he didn't have any substantive duties to fulfill and was no longer a contributing member to his department, but also very disconcerting to his wife as well. She had to bear her own frustrations over Gary's past decisions, which in moments of despair seemed reckless and not thoroughly thought out, given the consequences of his actions. Still, she continued to be supportive and understanding. So the decision was made: Gary would accept the university's offer, continue his part-time teaching, and begin the search for another job, preferably within the higher educational realm.

The Last Mile
chapter nine

Leaving the university was bittersweet. On the one hand, it was a painful experience to have severed ties with the institution after struggling for years to gain entry into that system, only to be shattered because of his philosophical commitment toward social justice. On the other hand, a heavy burden was lifted and he felt whole again, given that he had a year to resume his search in hopes of finding another position in higher education, only this time within the community college system, where he thought his best chance of being hired was, given his experience.

In the meantime, to keep busy so as not to become too restless and annoying to his family, Gary spent a considerable amount of time volunteering his services at one of the Chicano community organizations that had given their support during the 1980 demonstration. This organization was involved with social issues in connection with helping minorities and disadvantaged individuals secure employment, housing, and other social amenities.

As a volunteer, Gary was allowed use of the organization's facilities to continue his job search.

Several months had passed since leaving the university, so Gary was beginning to feel concerned about the possibility of not finding another position in higher education before the family's finances were exhausted. By this time he had submitted his résumé throughout the state's community college system but to no avail. Either he received rejections or no response at all. Not once did he ever come close to being granted an interview, though there were many position vacancies he applied for that he was well qualified to fill. It seemed as though, he thought, his reputation preceded him, given that there had been extensive coverage by the media of the 1980 demonstrations—his picture with several students on the front page of the newspaper, labeling him an "activist."

Working at the university had been a dream come true that ended as a nightmare, something Gary would have to live with until he could get back on his feet. Based on his attempts, however, landing another position within the college system seemed futile. He was now faced with the realization that regaining entry into a higher educational setting where he could continue helping minority and disadvantaged students achieve their goals may not ever come to fruition.

As more months passed, Gary extended his job search to include the four-year colleges throughout the state, but still he faced more rejections. *What next?* he thought. *Where do I go from here? Do I have to further my search to other parts of the country? Does it mean moving my family, again, to who knows where? Or do I have to humble myself and move back to Denver and live with my mother again until I find something suitable?* These were questions that Gary struggled with day and night; he had to do something soon about his situation to support his family. The monetary compensation he had received from the university was close to being depleted. So he extended his job search again, but only this time, throughout the country, including Colorado, which would be a welcoming site for his family. But like before, the rejection letters from the out-of-state colleges flowed in, with one exception: he had yet to hear back from one of the community colleges in Denver. *I guess my future in higher education is not to be,* Gary thought. *So I guess it's time I look around for other job opportunities outside the field of higher education.*

Gary, once again, found himself struggling with his demons, trying to overcome his frustrations. Depression factored into the equation, which Gary had experienced before. It caused him great concern, though he tried hiding it from his family. A few more weeks had passed and Gary was becoming increasingly worried about his situation. His depression seemed to be getting worse, and all he could think of was that he was failing his family and would never again have an opportunity like the one he had at the university. The negativity circling his mind was reinforcing his self-doubt and was not helpful. He finally realized he was facing reality in its raw form, so he turned to the only source that had seemingly lifted his parents out of the slums and into the housing projects. He put his troubles in God's hands and started attending daily Mass, trying to ease the emotional pain that had taken over his life and trying not to give up hope.

Then, as if a light switch turned on, Gary finally received a response from the community college in Denver where he had applied, inviting him to come in for an interview. The title was director of Student Affairs, a position he was qualified to fill and one that seemed like a perfect fit, given his extensive background. Advantages that Gary had were his knowledge of the campus and his acquaintances with several of the college's administrators, whom he had met years earlier while helping high school students gain entry into college after graduation. So he was excited and hopeful of his chance of being hired.

Things are now looking up (no pun intended), Gary thought as he sat next to the window on a 747, as he flew to Denver for a long-awaited job interview. Looking out over the snow-covered Cascade mountains as the plane flew over Washington State and then began its descent, two and a half hours later, over the equally snowcapped Rocky Mountains, flashbacks of all he had put his family through since leaving the oil company were heavy on his mind. *It's been a long journey,* he thought, *and hopefully this time, if hired, will be the last mile traveled toward securing a livelihood for my family.*

Once in Denver, Gary was looking forward to visiting with family and friends. He referred to Denver as home since it was always in the back of his mind that someday he and his family would return permanently. Gary's stay in Denver would be short, so he made a point to visit as many family members as possible; it had been three years since his last visit. During his visits he mostly stayed with two of his sisters; they were very attentive and loving, as were his other siblings, who also showed kindness. Every time Gary was in town, friends he had known since fourth grade through high school would gather for breakfast or dinner and talk about old times. There had always been a strong camaraderie among Gary and his childhood friends—Paul, John, Gerry, and Sal—who to this day remain close. Suffice it to say, Gary was pampered as if royalty each time he visited home.

As Gary approached the college campus, on his way to the interview, he noticed how beautiful it was, nestled against the foothills just outside the city, with a magnificent view of the mountains. There was a chill in the air and a light snow had covered the campus grounds as Gary walked toward the main entrance, holding on to an envelope with his résumé and additional reference letters inside. Entering the building, he walked somewhat nervously down the corridor toward the reception desk, saying to himself, *It's going to be okay. Just be yourself. Settle down.* After all, it had been nearly eight years since Gary had interviewed for a position.

"Good morning," Gary said to the receptionist as he introduced himself. "I'm here to see Mr. Morgan."

"Yes, sir," the receptionist answered. "Mr. Morgan is expecting you. Please have a seat and I will call him."

"Thank you," Gary said.

He took a seat next to a window with a view of the campus, and as he sat there, he had flashbacks of his meetings with the admissions and financial aid administrators back when he was helping high school students apply to college. His reminiscing of the past conjured up the positive relationships he had established with the college officials in the state of Colorado; he was hopeful this would be an asset toward his being considered for the position. One bothersome thought that could be a deal breaker, and in fact may have played a significant factor for all the rejection letters he'd received the past year, was the stance he chose to take against the UW that contributed to the student demonstrations of 1980.

"Gary, is that you?" asked a gentleman in a suit, walking down the hall.

"Bob," Gary replied. "Yes, it is. How are you? It's been a long time."

"Yes, it has," Bob answered. "I take it you're here for an interview for the director of Student Affairs position."

"Yes, I am."

"Well, good luck!" Bob said. "Come and see me after the interview so we can chat, and I'll bring you up to date as to what's going on these days."

"I'd like that," Gary said as his friend walked away.

Just then another gentleman approached Gary while stretching out his arm to shake Gary's hand. "Mr. Trujillo, I'm Bill Morgan. Let's go to my office."

"Good morning, sir. It's nice to meet you," Gary said.

Once in Mr. Morgan's office, they both sat on a long brown leather sofa and shared pleasantries while drinking coffee, after which the conversation turned more professional and focused on the student affairs position.

"Tell me, Mr. Trujillo, what interested you about the position, what is your management style, and how would you handle disgruntled employees because of an internal policy change in student admissions?" At that moment and just for an instant, maybe it was paranoia or just a coincidence that the question of an admissions policy change was posed, Gary could not help but think that his chance of being selected for the student affairs position was now in peril, that his past had preceded his visit, given the number of times he received rejection letters from the other colleges and universities he had applied to. Or perhaps this interview was merely a formality to demonstrate a good faith effort by the college regarding its Affirmative Action program. *But then on the other hand,* he thought. *No, I wouldn't have even been considered for this position had the college been aware of my involvement at the university. I must think positively about this opportunity I've been given and stop with the paranoia.* Gary then proceeded to answer the questions put forth, without hesitation, and was forthright with his answers.

"First, what interested me," Gary responded, "was the opportunity to return to Colorado, which was always my goal, and to hold a position as an administrator in a higher educational setting made up of students from diverse ethnic backgrounds, and to provide the leadership necessary to guide and direct them toward reaching their educational goals. Also, I have always been interested in the community college system, not only because of its diversity but because of its open-door admissions policy designed to reach out to both high school graduates and everyday working adults, offering short-term certification educational programs in the trades as well as two-year academic degrees.

"Second, with regard to my management style as it

relates to student affairs, I'm of the school of thought which encourages employee input in the decision-making process when it comes to dealing with major issues that may have a negative effect on working conditions or situations that could seriously impact student services negatively. It's the employees themselves who work directly with students and have a greater understanding of their needs and/or concerns that would be helpful to the administration. Employee collaboration, if you will.

"And third, as to how I would approach disgruntled employees because of an internal policy change in student admissions ties in with my answer to your second question regarding management style. I would, upon being hired, have ongoing discussions with the employees to discuss their concerns about the change they are reacting to and how it is impacting student admissions with regard to recruitment and enrollment. Then, after gathering and evaluating admissions data in an effort to determine, if in fact, the change in policy is having a negative effect on student recruitment and enrollment and is incongruent with the college's open-door policy, I would bring the matter to the attention of higher management for further review. I'm of the mind that to prevent employee grumbling, when it comes to making changes of any sort that may impact how they do their work, management needs to find a way to get them to respond in a proactive way rather than have them react negatively after changes have occurred."

After a few follow-up questions and back-and-forth discussion about the student affairs position and the college in general, the interview ended. Gary was then invited to lunch in the faculty lounge, followed by a tour of the campus. By this time he was feeling a little more at ease and mildly optimistic about his chance of being hired; things were not as dire as he first imagined, so he decided just to appreciate the moment and accept whatever was meant to be. After all, the fact that he landed an interview after receiving all those rejection letters gave him hope that there was "light at the end of the tunnel." After lunch, Gary thanked Mr. Morgan and returned to the receptionist desk to ask to see his friend whom he had run into earlier that morning. Gary was told he had left the campus for a meeting that was rescheduled for the afternoon.

The next three days flew by and Gary was back in Seattle, waiting to hear about the director of Student Affairs position. Three weeks passed and still no response from the college, so Gary called his friend there, who told him a decision had not yet been made; the competition was stiff but not to worry, he was one of the candidates still being considered, which gave Gary some comfort. A few more days went by and still no response from the college, at which point Gary was beginning to give up hope of ever finding permanent employment, let alone a position in higher education. And then it happened. As Gary was moping around the house, feeling sorry for himself, there was a knock on the door. And there stood the mailman with a certified letter, which needed to be signed for. Gary pushed open the screen door, signed for the letter, and slowly backed into the house, looking down at the letter to see whom the sender was. "Nance?" he yelled out. "It came."

"What came?" his wife asked.

"The letter from the college. It's finally here. Here, you open it," Gary said, walking into the kitchen where his wife was cleaning beans for dinner that evening.

"No, you open it. It's addressed to you. And if it's bad news, remember, it's not the end of the world."

Taking a deep breath, Gary opened the envelope, pulled out the letter, and began to read.

> Dear Mr. Trujillo:
>
> After further consideration of your application and personal interview for the position of director of Student Affairs, the decision was made to hire another candidate who the entire review board felt was more qualified. Thank you for the time and effort you put forth in what was a grueling process to fill the student affairs position. I wish you success in your further endeavors toward your career goal in higher education.
>
> Sincerely,
> Bill Morgan, Dean of Student Affairs

"Wow, another rejection letter," Gary said, his wife standing near him.

"I'm sorry, honey," his wife said. "I know this job meant a lot to you and to me as well. I was kind of looking forward to moving back home. You can't just give up, though. Something will come up, you'll see. Then again, maybe we're just meant to make Seattle our home.

It is beautiful here, you know," she said with a smile. "Besides, you're the one who always said, 'Never give up.' Well then, don't give up. Stay strong."

"Yeah, you're right. Again!" Gary said jokingly as he kissed his wife on the cheek and went out into the backyard.

Over the next two months Gary kept himself busy, volunteering his time at the Chicano organization, helping with some of the community outreach services, while still sending out employment inquiries. Then one day the director of the organization approached Gary and said that the president of the United Farm Workers of America, Cesar Chavez, was coming to Seattle and would Gary like to be his driver during his stay? They needed someone to take him to several scheduled community events and to the various media outlets. The purpose of his visit was to inform the public of the devastating effects that pesticides, used by the growers, were having on farmworkers. Cesar Chavez was nationally known throughout the United States and around the world for his undying commitment to helping farmworkers remain safe while working in the produce fields of North America. Cesar's entire adult life, until his death at the age of sixty-six, was spent working toward helping farmworkers and their families receive a decent living wage, livable conditions throughout the labor camps, and health benefits, all of which were dependent upon successful negotiations with the growers.

Driving Cesar Chavez and two of his organizers that accompanied him that week, for Gary, was an honor and a privilege. Gary had first learned of Cesar's reputation in the late 1960s and was impressed by his commitment to the farmworker. While seeing to it that Cesar reached his intended audiences, Gary felt a sense of calm and peace while in his presence. He couldn't explain it, but it was as though all the pressure he was under at the time to find a job had vanished. Being in Cesar's presence, a man of worldly notoriety due to his tireless work on behalf of the nation's produce harvesters, was an overwhelming experience for Gary. Yet, on the other hand, being around Cesar and his companions that week was like hanging out with close friends. There were moments of laughter, kidding around, and enjoying each other's company.

The second time Gary had the opportunity to be around Cesar Chavez was during the summer of 1986, when he took part in a twenty-mile walk from Toppenish to Yakima to support the farmworker movement in Washington State. Despite the circumstances surrounding the plight of farmworkers, there was a sense of joy and excitement among the two hundred marchers as they sang traditional Mexican songs while cheering and waiving at bypassers. This was not only a new experience for Gary but memorable one as well. Though at one point he had to borrow a pair of shoes from a friend to complete the march.

It had now been nearly a year since Gary left the university and, once again, he was feeling the pressure with no end in sight. His financial situation had dwindled and his depression set in. Each day seemed to get worse. And his praying hadn't produced any answers. He felt lost and hopeless of ever finding a job, and it was no secret to his wife how he was feeling. So she asked, "What do you think of me going back to work? Mark's mother said they were hiring where she works, and if I was interested, she could help me get a job and we could ride together. The hours, however, are from three p.m. to midnight, so I'm going to need help with the boys. What do you think?"

"I think you need to do it. Things aren't getting any better, and we need the income. The way things are, I don't know when I'm going to start working again."

It had been twenty years since Gary's wife had worked. The year they were married she was working at the telephone company, her first job after graduating high school. Then, after their first child was born, she worked one more year and never worked again outside the home. Going back to work was going to take some adjustment. She had a lot of confidence in herself, and once she started working, her determination to help their situation at home grew stronger. So, after working a few months assembling circuit boards, she decided to look for another job with better health benefits, working conditions, and wages. Then, within a short time, she secured a job at Safeway, where she retired from twenty-six years later.

It was not only an adjustment for Gary's wife to reenter the job market, but quite an adjustment for Gary as well. Since the time he and his wife were married, Gary had never really paid much attention to what it took to maintain a household, not to mention the care that was demanded in raising three kids, who by now were teenagers. It was now his turn to take on more of the responsibility of daily housekeeping and supervision of their three sons by seeing to it they were well cared for and that they went to school on time. At times Gary had to physically pull them out of bed feet first or splash water on their face to get them to respond. Their youngest, Donald, attended Catholic grade school and carpooled with other kids in the neighborhood, while his two older sons, Eric and Christopher, attended public high school after completing Catholic grade school. It was during this time that Gary had established a stronger bond with his sons which continue to exist.

Now that Gary's wife was employed, he felt a great sense of relief and knew that their situation was about to change for the better. *My prayers are being answered,* he thought. *Maybe not all of them but some.* Gary had tried placing his trust in God and developed a strong devotion to the Blessed Mother—thanks to his mother, who served as an example in raising seven children and supporting them along with her husband, a chronic alcoholic, while working full-time, at night, as a nurse aide at a Catholic hospital.

Thinking back about how his mother survived and the devotion she had toward the Blessed Mother reminded him of a statue of the Blessed Mother he had seen at a Catholic bookstore; he wanted to buy it and place it in his backyard. One of his very close childhood friends had a statue of Our Lady in his backyard, and that image had always been in the back of his mind. The cost of the statue was $400, though $200 would hold it until the full price could be paid. However, Gary could not even afford the $200, so he put the thought behind him.

The next few months passed, and by this time Gary had established a regular routine at home. He was now, officially, a full-time stay-at-home husband, father, and housekeeper, though not a very good one. And for the first time since his sons were born, his concept of marriage was fully realized.

While still volunteering at the Chicano organization, Gary was approached by the organization's director, who handed him a check for $200. When asked why, he was told it was considered a stipend for the training he had conducted earlier for teachers who were interested in learning about minority community organizations. The stipend was a total surprise and a pleasant one at that. Now Gary was able to make the down payment on the statue of the Blessed Mother. *Another prayer answered,* he thought. *Now all I need is $200 and She's mine.* As it turned out, once Gary informed his wife of the payment he had received and what he had done with it, she give him the remaining $200 he needed to pay the balance. That following week Gary brought the statue home and placed it in cement in the backyard, where he had constructed a grotto, to protect the statue during high winds.

In October 1986 at the church where Gary and his family had been attending since 1978, they started the Perpetual Adoration, which is a display of devotion toward our Lord by a parishioner who spends every hour of the day, 365 days a year, in prayer. A practice which Gary and his wife have been doing for more than thirty years now.

Gary continued his search for employment, and in

Statue of Mary and grotto in author's backyard.

the process, turned to a close friend he and his wife had known for many years, who lived in Denver and worked for the government, to see if he could help him find a position in government service. For the longest time Gary had no interest in government service and avoided applying for those jobs. His only reason was based on feedback from friends he knew who worked for the government in different capacities and talked negatively about their experience; the environment was cold, secretive, insensitive toward minorities, and exuded a sense of paranoia. *I guess I'm just going to have to swallow my pride,* Gary thought. At that moment he flashed back to the time he found himself faced with a similar dilemma, when he asked to be rehired at the oil company after quitting because he thought he could do better elsewhere, which never materialized. Hence his outreach to his friend—who, it just so happened, used to work with the director of a federal agency in Seattle—and arranged a meeting for them to discuss employment possibilities. In the meantime, another friend of Gary's, who also worked for the government, said his agency was hiring and that Gary should apply; he knew the regional manager and would put in a good word for Gary.

Now it seemed there was a glimmer of hope. Gary had two job prospects and his spirits were lifted. So the next two weeks he spent preparing his application for government service, which turned out to be a lengthy process. Unlike preparing separate job applications for other government and private sector jobs, the federal government required an enormous employment application applicable for multiple government agencies. Upon completing his application and sending it to both federal agencies, Gary met with the two individuals referred to him by his friends and learned what the jobs entailed. The agency that was more appealing to Gary, because it dealt with helping minority small-business owners gain access to government contracts, it turned out, was under a hiring freeze, and there was no telling when the freeze would be lifted. The other agency dealt with government compliance regarding employment regulations, but the job was temporary. However, Gary was in no position to be choosy, so if offered the position he would accept it. After all, it had been fourteen months since he last held a job, so he was excited to get back to work.

As it turned out, Gary was hired to fill the temporary position, which involved conducting site visits at large private corporations to determine if federal compliance laws were being met regarding hiring practices, including promotions, and other employee personnel actions pertaining to minorities and women in connection with the Affirmative Action program—an instrument of the federal government used to ensure equal treatment of employees. Then a collateral duty was thrown into the mix, addressing employment discrimination claims by individuals with physical disabilities. While the job was a new experience, working to address the inequities suffered by disadvantaged individuals was an area of intense interest to Gary, given his past experience working to enhance the upward mobility of minorities. Faced with a new challenge, Gary would expand his knowledge and experience, adding to his marketability toward future promotional opportunities within government service.

Toward the end of 1986, on Thanksgiving Day, and after nearly a year and a half of struggling to find a job, Gary's confidence was back. He had just started a job with the federal government, his wife was working, he was still teaching part-time, and his longtime dream of having a statue of the Blessed Mother in his backyard had come true. *What more could I ask for?* he thought. *My prayers have been answered.* The pressure Gary was under and the depression he experienced had all faded. Now he was, once again, fully relaxed, happy, and content with life.

While Thanksgiving dinner was being prepared, Gary

received a call from the director of the Chicano organization. He told Gary that Cesar Chavez was in town again, accompanied by two of his organizers, and would he pick them up and take them to where they would be staying for the next few days? Cesar would also need someone to drive him to his scheduled events as before. Without giving it another thought, Gary was on his way to pick them up.

While visiting Seattle, Cesar Chavez stayed with the Sisters of Providence, a small community of Catholic nuns; they had prepared a room for him in their home overlooking Lake Washington. On the day of his visit, however, the nuns happened to not be home, so Gary invited Cesar and his companions to Thanksgiving dinner with him and his family; after dinner, he would take Cesar back to the Sisters' home and his companions to where they were staying.

Gary would often comment to family and friends that having Cesar Chavez sit at the table with him and his family that Thanksgiving Day was a special occasion and an honor to have a man of such stature in their presence; all he ate was vegetables while everyone else enjoyed a full Thanksgiving dinner with all the trimmings. It deserves repeating that Cesar Chavez was a man who had dedicated his life trying to see to it that farmworkers, the very people responsible for harvesting the food put on the tables of millions of Americans, were treated with dignity and respect, and that their work in the fields, under the hot sun, day after day, would earn them a fair wage most Americans take for granted. Cesar Chavez was a man who had directed the attention of presidents, politicians, and the entire country, if not the world, toward an unjust system subjecting the farmworker to a lower standard of living.

That following week, Gary had the privilege again of driving Cesar Chavez to prearranged meetings with various community activist groups to elicit their support in spreading the word of the danger pesticides, used by farm owners, posed to farmworkers. Gary was especially impressed by Cesar's spirituality. Part of his daily schedule consisted of attending Mass, which Gary attributed to the peacefulness he felt when in his presence.

The year 1986 was coming to an end, and Gary was gradually settling into his new job of two months when he was notified that the hiring freeze at the other federal agency he was interested in would soon be lifted, if he was still interested in a position. Gary was surprised and happy to hear the news and so expressed his interest. However, he would have to submit a detailed statement specific to the position he would be applying for and it would take a few weeks before hearing back, given the government's hiring process. Then by mid-March, the following year, Gary received a letter from the agency stating he was one of the finalists for the position of small-business specialist. In the meantime, Gary had not mentioned to his supervisor or the district director who had hired him that he had also applied to work at another government agency. However, since there were no guaranties he would be hired, he decided to wait until he heard, for sure, if he got the job before going forward with any news.

A week later, Gary was notified he had been selected

for the small-business specialist position to take effect in two weeks. Now Gary had to give notice of his departure, and when he did, his district director was greatly disappointed and showed it by the way in which he reacted to the news. After which, however, he understood Gary's decision to leave and wished him well. After all, the job Gary was taking was permanent and at a higher grade level, which meant of course, a higher salary. By the end of March 1987, Gary, once again, was in his element working to help minorities achieve upward mobility. This time, however, it was in the area of business development, another challenge he looked forward to facing.

Over the next twenty-three years Gary worked in government service, providing business development and contract assistance to minority small-business owners engaged in manufacturing, construction, sales, and service industries. The government provided all the necessary training to effectively carry out the demands and challenges of the job by offering year-round classes throughout different parts of the country that included management, accounting/bookkeeping, human relations, marketing, financial analysis, and government contracting.

By the time Gary had reached his ninth year on the job, he not only completed the required basic training classes but also took advanced government contracting classes, thus earning a certification as a contracting officer (CO). As a CO, he was authorized to sign multimillion-dollar contracts and interact directly with government contracting officers throughout the country when it came to helping his clients bid and negotiate government contracts. Now Gary held two job titles. Also, during this time period, after eighteen months of being on the job, Gary was promoted to director of business development, responsible for supervising four employees and overseeing program operations. And within a few months of his promotion, he was presented the District Director's Excellence Award.

Then in 1995, the agency underwent an organizational change that affected the way in which it was structured. The regional office in each state was significantly downsized, causing personnel reassignments throughout the country. As a result of this action, the regional director of business development was reassigned to the district office as director of business development, thus bumping Gary back down to the position of a business specialist, which he held until the day he retired (December 2010). Though Gary was terribly disappointed and angry and had formed a negative attitude toward management, because he felt he had been treated unfairly, he still retained his grade level and, in time, accepted his role in the organization.

It was another godsend, he would later believe. Although at the time, and for a couple of years afterward, he didn't think so. Eventually, he came to the realization that all the anger and negative feelings he had stored up inside were not healthy or productive. In fact, his negative disposition had alienated some of his co-workers, who kept their distance from him so as not to give management the impression they had taken sides. So he decided that if he was going to survive this last chapter of his professional career and retire in good health, he needed to change his attitude and form a positive outlook to reframe his professional story.

Over the next several years and until his retirement, Gary reestablished his excellent reputation as a hardworking, dedicated employee. He mended his relationship with upper management and soon was considered a valuable asset by his immediate supervisor, the person who bumped him from his directorship, to help her meet the department's yearly goals and advance their regional standing. Their close working relationship continued until she retired.

After which, Gary applied for the position he once held, though he knew his chances of being selected were not good, given the history. He just wanted management to know of his interest in managing the division again. Also, it was common knowledge that the district director wanted to hire someone outside the immediate area to fill the position, so it wasn't a great disappointment when he was not selected. He instead put the matter behind him and continued focusing on performing his daily responsibilities while establishing an excellent working relationship with the new director of business development.

To add to his many accomplishments since graduating high school, serving in the military, and earning undergraduate and graduate degrees, Gary became a business owner himself when he bought a restaurant while still holding down a full-time job with the government. The year was 2001, and Gary had been with the government for over thirteen years. Now he experienced the ins and outs of business ownership.

The way in which it all came about was through his

eldest son, Eric, who worked for his best friend's father, who owned a Mediterranean restaurant near the Puget Sound. The owner was looking to retire and wanted to sell the business. Not knowing anything about running a business, let alone a restaurant, Gary purchased it on behalf of his son, whose idea it was, in the first place, to go into the restaurant business.

The next four and a half years became an exhausting reality for Gary. He was not only working full-time at his day job but also washing dishes in the evenings and maintaining the grounds around the restaurant, pulling weeds, trimming hedges, and keeping the parking lot free of debris. Not to mention his responsibilities at home. The rest of the time he kept busy recording expenditures and sales, making payroll, paying business taxes, and handling other business-related matters, such as securing financing to supplement income needed to maintain operations since daily sales were not sufficient enough to realize a profit.

Now Gary had a taste of what it was like trying to maintain a business and the enormous responsibility and time it took to remain operational. In a strange way, Gary enjoyed his predicament and found owning a business "romantic," though challenging. The sad part, however, was that after all the time, effort, and financing invested to hold on to the business, it became a losing proposition. The revenue generated was just not enough to keep the doors open. So on New Year's Eve 2004, Gary closed the business. *All in all, it was a bittersweet experience,* he thought, as the romanticism of owning a business slowly faded. After closing the business, Gary had a deeper appreciation of what small-business owners go through on a daily basis just to survive.

Gary was always looking for something new to do that would enhance the way in which he performed his job. It was never enough, it seemed, just to do what was basically required. In an effort, therefore, to enhance what his job description entailed, Gary took it upon himself to expand his duties by designing a cost proposal training class to help the clients deal with the complexities of working with the government. The training class dealt specifically with how to structure government bids with regard to direct and indirect costs, overhead and profit, and what constituted fair and reasonable pricing.

Gary had become the resident expert in government contracting in his district and soon found himself helping other agency co-workers throughout the region. He was even asked by an outside business organization to accompany them to several cities throughout the states of Washington and Idaho to offer his training class to other small-business owners engaged in government contracting. Once again, he found life on the job enjoyable and exciting.

Gary worked six more years helping minority small-business owners navigate through the government's contracting maze. On Thursday evening, December 30, 2010, Gary left the office for the last time, got on a bus to go home. Looking back on his twenty-seven years in government service, including the military, motivated him to write this book for family and friends, and possibly the public, should there be an interest in *Little Gary's Journey.*

The following week (January 5, 2011), Gary started a small-business consulting service, helping small-business owners through the federal government's contracting process, and other related business matters, which he operates to this day.

Epilogue

At the age of seventy-five and eight years into my retirement, and after closing out the last chapter of this book I started writing thirty-eight years ago, I find myself, again, sitting back, though not in a plush velvet swivel chair but rather in the massage recliner my wife gave me as a retirement gift. This time I'm at home in our family room, looking out to the backyard at the beautiful statue of the Blessed Mother I purchased back in 1986 and thanking Her for intervening, on my behalf, with her Son, to guide and protect me throughout life.

As I sit here, I can't help but reflect again on the impoverished conditions I faced as a young child growing up in government housing with my parents, three older sisters, and three younger brothers. My thoughts are about the happy and sad times of my life, the discipline imposed on me by my father, the love my mother displayed in her quiet manner, the church's moral teachings, and the love and support of my wife and three sons. And most vividly, the many paths I took that led me to this moment of great satisfaction and appreciation for all that I have.

All of what I have experienced during my lifetime I consider blessings in disguise, making it possible for me to navigate through life's struggles by overcoming rejection and disappointment to achieve the rewards and benefits I enjoy today. In essence, these elements in my life were the ingredients for who I am and what I believe in. Most important, they are what strengthened my faith in God.

Now that my life, from childhood to adulthood, is fully laid out in story form, my nine grandchildren and future great-grandchildren will have an opportunity to learn more about who their grandfather was and the challenges and struggles I faced, for the sake of my family, to overcome life's obstacles. While it was persistence that held me up as I walked through life's maze, it was my faith that shielded me from the dark side of life.

My sons are grown now with families of their own. My high school sweetheart wife and I have had the luxury of traveling within and outside the country. Both my parents have passed: my father at an early age of liver disease from drinking too much; my mother of heart failure at seventy-eight. She remained single until her death in 1994. Two of my brothers have also died, Donny from gun violence at the age of twenty-two, and Paul from cancer just prior to the release of this book. My remaining siblings, Cindy, Frances, Margaret, and Danny live with their families in Denver. Also, two of my close friends, Roy from my early childhood, and Dwayne, my high school classmate and best man at my wedding, died at an early age. Now Nancy and I are enjoying the fruits of our labor and keeping our weekly visits of adoration we started thirty-two years ago.

"Well, what are you thinking about now, sitting there, staring out the window? Your book is finished, so you don't need to daydream about the past anymore. I've called for you several times and you haven't responded. Dinner's on the table. We're having beans. And for dessert, we're sharing a Hostess CupCake."

Acknowledgments

Little Gary's Journey would have never become a reality had it not been for the love, encouragement, and support of family and friends, who, over the past thirty-eight years, were constant reminders to keep "Little Gary" alive. The idea of an autobiography surfaced when my staff and I discussed growing up, while I was director of the Chicano Student Services division at the University of Washington, in the late 1970s and '80s. We shared where we grew up, the hardships we had faced, and what brought us to our present situations. From these discussions, I began writing about an episode of my life I experienced at the age of seven, having to do with two cream-filled cupcakes. It was that story, "Hostess CupCake," I credit to my brother Paul, who inspired me to continue writing. When he read the only page I had at that time, in my amateurish attempt at writing, he got choked up and said, as he tried holding back his emotions, "Damn, Gary, you have to keep writing." Thank you, brother.

Since that touching moment, it has taken me many

years to chronicle my life, and there have been many individuals who've played a significant role in how my life has been shaped and who deserve acknowledgment, some of whom have since passed but will never be forgotten. First and foremost is my lovely wife, Nancy, of fifty-two years, and our three sons, Eric, Christopher, and Donald, who bore the brunt of the decisions I made, which at times caused undue hardship in our life, but who never gave up on me. Second, are my siblings and their families, who always showed an interest when I brought up "Little Gary" and discussed what my intentions were in going forward with the story. Others in my life who came to my rescue and lifted my spirits by guiding me back to the road of recovery, when I was floundering either because of uncontrollable circumstances or poor decisions I made, are John Dominquez, John Herrera, and Richard Gallegos, who were instrumental in helping me secure employment for me at critical times. Then there are my early childhood friends, Roy Alcon and Johnny Jacinto, both deceased, and Leonard Benavidez, with whom I've lost contact but think of often, who played a major part in my life prior to moving into the housing projects at the age of ten, and who are essential figures in *Little Gary's Journey* (Roy, Johnny, and Leonard). Next are two of my lifelong friends whom I've known since the fourth grade: Paul Baca, who helped me with the dialogue in my book in its earlier stage; and John Dominquez, who not only helped me gain employment on three separate occasions but also took the blame when I wrecked his father's car while driving my girlfriend Nancy home one snowy evening after a basketball game. I would also like to thank Michele (a.k.a. Mickie) Boyer, who did some editing for the first four chapters I had written at the time and encouraged me to continue. Then there is Peter Beaulieu, my friend from church, who made it all possible for me to finish this journey. After turning to him for guidance, given he is a published author, he not only took great interest in what I had written but helped me transition "Little Gary" to "Gary." I was stuck in a hole, and he lifted me out, and within six months I had written four additional chapters, nonstop, to bring closure to this autobiography.

Also, thanks to my sons Christopher and Donald, who contributed to making Little Gary's journey a reality—Christopher, for his constructive criticism when he reviewed sections, and Donald, along with his friend Jon Sternoff, for their creative ability in helping me design the books cover. Last but not least, thanks to my friend Steve Menard, who put me in touch with Jennifer Sugden, who performed a myriad of tasks associated with the packaging of my book, and who, in turn, introduced me to Carrie Wicks, who did the copyediting. I hope you enjoy my story.

www.ingramcontent.com/pod-product-compliance
Lightning Source LLC
Chambersburg PA
CBHW071357290426
44108CB00014B/1584